Finding
Joy
in Suffering

D1716313

A MEMOIR BY MEENA RIVERA

DEDICATION

This book is dedicated to the many families and friends who have shaped my life. First and foremost, to my mother, Darlene Dee Paes, this book is for you. Though our life together was brief, it was beautiful and full of so much love. Thank you for loving me so well and caring for me with your whole heart. I will cherish our memories in my heart forever.

Second, this book is written in memory of my dad, Orlando Rivera. Dad, thank you for adopting me and loving me as your daughter. You have shown me Christ in the most honorable and selfless ways. I will never forget your teachings and your humor. Thank you for helping me love my story by stepping into it with joy and devotion.

CONTENTS

INTRODUCTION

Finding Joy in Suffering. Quite a title, right? Usually, you wouldn't think that joy and suffering would exist together. But in my life, they have. I've experienced great suffering and loss early on in my life, and many have asked me how I continue to put a smile on my face having lived through what I have. Ever since I was a kid, my response has been, *"I don't know, it's because of Jesus."* For a while, I couldn't understand why I had joy in my heart after my mother died. But I knew that God was providing joy in ways that I couldn't begin to explain. Even now, so many years later, I can still say that I have joy in my seasons of suffering.

My story has been shaped by the loss of two of my parents. My birth mother died after a long battle with cancer when I was 12, and my adopted dad died from a fatal car accident when I was 25. I've suffered from depression for many years and struggled with suicide and self-harm. I've struggled with my mental health, a number of insecurities, and ongoing fears of rejection and abandonment. You name it, I, or someone I know, has struggled and suffered through something. I bet you have suffered in some way, shape, or form at least once in your life. Everyone suffers. No matter how small or large, insignificant, or grand, you have suffered.

This book may not teach you how to avoid suffering, because we can't avoid suffering. But it will teach you how to walk through it, and how to walk alongside someone else through theirs. Suffering is an unfortunate part of this world, and we will all experience some kind of suffering. But in order to do life on this earth (and find the joy in it), we need to first acknowledge and accept our suffering, and then get to know the One who suffered more than all of us. Jesus. And only then, will we be able to find a reason to have joy in the midst of our suffering.

I've been encouraged to write my story for many years, but it hasn't felt like the right time until now. This isn't your typical book, and you might be wondering, "Why a memoir?" Well, my story is a unique one, and I've learned a lot over the years, from my experiences with loss, about how to live life in this broken world. While I have suffered tragedy and heartbreaking losses, God has made those stories beautiful because of His

1

role in them. I wouldn't be where I am without God, and His saving grace, mercy, and love for me. I wouldn't get through the day and see everlasting joy on the other side without God.

As you embark on a journey through the first 26 years of my life, you'll get a brief window into a few significant stories that have shaped who I am. Many of my memories will read like a storybook for Parts 1 and 2 of this book, and Parts 3 and 4 of this book will read more as an introspective look at life with some significant memories sprinkled in. I've known suffering for most of my life, but God has stepped in and revealed His joy to me in so many ways.

I hope that as you read my story, you can begin to view your story differently, in light of what God has done in and through it. My wish is that you will start seeing your suffering as a gift from God. It may not make sense quite yet. But there is joy in your suffering too. God has written a beautiful story for you and even the hard, dark, and scary parts are beautiful. We have to view our story from God's perspective, and that will take time. But I hope you can glean some insights from what I've learned, so that you too can love your story and, in turn, walk alongside others in their suffering as well.

Love, Meena

PART I

1 THE BEGINNING

My story begins in the heart of Atlanta, Georgia, in a small delivery room at Northside Hospital in the year 1993, about three weeks before Christmas. I was born on December 3rd to Darlene Paes, a beautiful, strong willed, registered nurse. Our life began in Decatur, a fairly small suburban town outside of Atlanta, Georgia.

Many of the early years from my childhood feel like a faint blip in time. I have a cloudy jumble of memories, pieced together by old pictures with my mother's handwritten inscription on the back, describing what was going on in the photo. Even the photos my mother kept of me as a baby bring back vague recollections; from a time that feels very real, even if I can't piece together the events that took place when the photo was taken.

One memory I can vividly recall from her photos was my third birthday, on December 3rd, 1996. I remember celebrating with my preschool friends, all of us sitting around a small table in our classroom. I can picture everyone there, singing "happy birthday" to me. To this day, I believe it's one of my earliest memories, one of the best ones. My childhood had many happy memories, full of laughter and smiles, especially at school.

I started going to preschool when I was four months old in the spring of 1994, and my mother really showed her "mama bear" side to my preschool teachers. I was her first child and the most important person in her life; she never failed to let me know how much I meant to her.

There were a couple aspects of my infancy that contributed to her meticulous and highly protective care. First, my mother highly valued my health and safety, largely due to the fact that she was a registered nurse and a first-time single mom. Second, by my first birthday I had been diagnosed with cerebral palsy, partly because I wasn't showing any initiative to start walking. My mother was fearful that I would never be able to walk if this wasn't taken care of quickly. So, I was placed in weekly physical therapy for one year to work on my motor skills and range of motion. By my second birthday, I was showing great progress, surpassed my walking goals, and cerebral palsy was no longer a concern in my development. Since my mother's desire for me to exceed and surpass developmental goals didn't stop there, so excelling in school quickly became a main focus at home.

My mother valued education over everything. Therefore, our relationship was a unique one. I always knew how much she cared about me and how much she loved me; but in those early years our relationship seemed to be defined by how well I did in school. She worked long hours as a nurse, so I wasn't able to see her often during the week. Our limited time together in the evenings was primarily focused on practicing my reading and writing. As she strongly encouraged excellence in my schooling, in time I also grew to appreciate and value becoming an exceptional student and maintaining perfect grades.

In the seasons when school was out for the holidays, my mother always made an effort to have fun with me and plan trips for us. We would spend the holidays in Savannah, Georgia, get all dressed up, go out to dinner, and see all the lights during Christmastime. Though it was just the two of us, all that mattered was that we were together.

———————————————

In 2001, a lot of change was brewing for my mother and me. Little did I know at the time, this was our last year in Georgia. At the end of second grade, my elementary school announced that they would be making some changes to their curriculum and would no longer be offering Spanish classes. Since entering Kindergarten, I had been part of the Spanish magnet program and had loved getting to learn Spanish each year. For my mother, it was incredibly important for me to learn a second language in school, so thus began the hunt for another school before the fall semester began. My mother was quite the adventurer and free spirit, so once it was clear that I needed a change in my education and environment, she had all the momentum needed to mix up our lifestyle.

In the summer of 2002, my mother and I packed up our things, said goodbye to our friends, and moved to Orlando, Florida. It was hard to leave all of my friends and Decatur behind, they were the only people and place I had ever known, but it was time for us both to move on. That fall was the beginning of a new adventure for us.

Welcome to the Sunshine State

In July of 2002, my mother and I began the next season of our lives in Florida. We moved to a quaint neighborhood less than a ten-minute drive from Downtown Orlando. I'll never forget our first house, it was this pink pastel colored two-bedroom, two-bathroom. In the front yard next to our driveway, there stood one large, tall tree, flush with leaves that always left a pile beneath its branches in the fall. I remember spending hours sitting under that tree, watching the clouds, as the breeze blew around me and helped cool off the humid afternoons.

The inside our house was a little more chaotic. My mother loved to keep everything we owned, so the entire time we lived there we were never fully unpacked, but it was home. We spent most of our time together relaxing in the living room, watching tennis, basketball, the Olympics, or old James Bond films. My room was on the first floor, where I could have the entire downstairs to play and make my own. My mother's room was upstairs, and many nights I'd sleep with her, because I was often afraid to sleep downstairs by myself. I didn't mind though, getting to cuddle up with my mother was always my favorite.

Late August of 2002, I began attending a new elementary school. They had an amazing magnet program for accelerated learning and, of course, a Spanish program. I adjusted fairly well to my new school and began to make new friends. I kept myself busy with many after school activities, including joining the swim team at the Downtown YMCA, taking piano lessons, and occasionally volunteering at my mother's job at a nursing home, serving dinner to the elderly. My mother's work schedule didn't keep her working too late this time, so we were able to spend more evenings together.

Our first summer in Orlando was life changing for us both. I remember it was the last day of school, and I had just finished third grade. I was standing outside the front of my school and found a flyer promoting a Vacation Bible School open to anyone in the community. It mentioned that a few local churches were all participating, and I thought it would be a lot of fun to attend camp for the summer. I had no idea that it was a Christian camp, and up until this point my mother and I had never discussed faith or religion in our house. I had no idea who God was or what Christianity was at all, but attending camp and getting to hang out with other kids was all the reason I needed to try it out.

I remember on the first day of VBS being really nervous about not knowing anyone. I was an incredibly shy nine-year-old, but three girls (all sisters) came up to me in the registration line, immediately introduced themselves, and said they would show me around. I was placed in their group, and we got to hang out all week long. During the very last group session on the last day, the speaker gave an encouraging message to all of the kids and asked if anyone wanted to accept Jesus into their hearts. As I sat in my seat, my heart beating fast, I knew that this message was for me. I loved that the pastor spoke about how God doesn't ask us to be perfect. We don't have to do anything to earn His love or to earn our salvation. We just have to believe in Him, confess our sins, and accept Him into our hearts. For me, this was a significant realization; one that my childlike heart could actually understand and believe to be the best news I had ever heard.

You see, throughout my years in elementary school, I had grown up believing that excelling in school was the most important thing in my life. Every day after school, I would keep a record of how often I did something wrong that day. When I believed that I wasn't a good kid, I would tell myself that I needed to be better next time. I would strive, with as much sheer will as I could muster, to be my very best, to be better, the next day. And I remember each day, when I would fail to be my best, I would get so frustrated and disappointed in myself, realizing that I had messed up again. So, to know that God still loved me even though I constantly failed, even though I wasn't perfect; that changed my life completely. I didn't have to be perfect to be accepted by Christ, and that was beautiful for my little ears to hear. From that moment on, if I made a mistake in life, I could ask for forgiveness and truly be forgiven by God. I remember standing up boldly when the leader of the camp asked hundreds of kids if they wanted to accept Christ. And I proudly said yes, and asked Jesus into my heart; believing in Him and knowing that I would follow Him for the rest of my life. That was the day I became a Christian, and I knew my life would never be the same — it would be so much better because Jesus was in my heart forever.

As VBS came to a close, my new friends introduced my mother and I to their whole family. They had three other brothers, and I learned that they were all adopted. The parents, Orlando and Nancy, had adopted six black kids of different ages, from different foster homes, with various difficult backgrounds. Their story was one filled with beauty and of God's provision. After my mother and I met the whole family, we were invited to attend their church, called the HUB Church. They met every Sunday at the Downtown YMCA; and Orlando was the pastor of the church.

My mother and I began attending church regularly that summer, and the HUB became our home church every Sunday that followed. I quickly stepped into volunteering in their nursery and in their Sunday-school classes; while my mother was encouraged to attend a bible study called *The Purpose Driven Life*, based on the book study by Rick Warren, which met weekly at Orlando and Nancy's home. The following spring, in February of 2004, my mother completed the Bible study and accepted Christ into her heart.

Many of you may not realize how momentous this decision was for my mother, accepting Christ into her heart and deciding to live her life solely for Him. But God knew it was time.

9

2 DARLENE

Let's rewind for a bit so I can give you a brief window into who my mother was before she had me.

Darlene was born on August 4th, 1961, in Wilmington, North Carolina to Doris and Darwin Paes. Darlene had a brother Butch and a sister Shirley (both from her mother's first marriage), and two nieces Donna and Lynn (Shirley's daughters). The Paes family lived in North Carolina briefly, then moved to Vermont for another short time, following wherever the United States Air Force stationed Darwin. After a few years, they finally settled in Refton, Pennsylvania.

When Darlene was only six years old, her mother died suddenly from a stroke. Then a couple years later, her father died unexpectedly from a pre-existing medical condition, leaving her without any parents. Her brother Butch was 22 and living out of the house by that time, but he couldn't take care of her. So, she went to live with her older sister, Shirley and her family in Laurel, Maryland. This was a rough adjustment as you can imagine, for a little girl to have lost both her parents at such a young age. Thankfully, Shirley's daughters, Donna and Lynn, were very close in age to Darlene, so they went to school together and grew very close to each other over time. Soon, Darlene began to see Donna and Lynn as her sisters, and Shirley as her mom.

When she grew into a young teenager, Darlene was a force of nature. She had wild, light brown, loosely curled hair that was always done up in that common 70's hairstyle, the "Farrah Fawcett flip". She also had about a million freckles all over, giving that extra edge of beauty to her fair skin. Darlene had a smile and laugh that captivated a room. She was the kind of woman who easily set herself apart from the crowd and knew who she was no matter what anyone said. Her independent personality complemented how headstrong and set in her ways she was; she wasn't afraid to be bold and say exactly what was on her mind.

Darlene was one of a kind to say the least. She liked crazy things, just to be different. She didn't care what anyone thought about her. But at the same time, she was constantly anxious, and her mind would run through "what ifs" all the time. She had a hard time living in the moment and was always looking for the next best thing in life. So, she worried about the future all of the time.

Darlene was also a typical teenager and always had her head in the clouds, but she made sure no one could see how she wore her heart on her sleeve. She had a high school sweetheart, and everyone thought they would be together forever. But their relationship ended in college with broken hearts and lost friendships. Darlene wasn't ready to commit to forever, but he was. So, as she moved on, she continued to pursue her nursing degree at UNC-W (University of North Carolina in Wilmington) with dreams of becoming a nurse practitioner and opening up her own private practice.

Darlene was never a conventional woman, so in her spare time she traveled all over the world (mostly Southeast Asia) and lived life the way she wanted. She had an adventurous spirit, wild and colorful, and worked hard at everything she did. She had such a passionate heart to see and experience everything the world had to offer.

She was obsessed with music and writing. She loved to write more than anything and would write pages and pages of notes in her journals, about anything and everything. The soundtrack to her life would be filled with records from the 70's and 80's. Back in high school, she'd play records on her turntable and just dance all around the house. She loved going to concerts and seeing her favorite artists play live. She loved Electric Light Orchestra, KC and the Sunshine Band, Elton John, Billy Joel, Fleetwood Mac, Journey, Beatles, ABBA, the Bee Gees, Osmond Brothers, Jackson 5, and many others. Her favorite song was "Build Me Up Buttercup" by the Temptations.

When my mother was 33 years old, she found out she was pregnant with only a slight idea of who my father might be. At the time, she was living as a nurse in Georgia and had very open relationships with a couple of guys. It wasn't until after I was born that she knew who of the two was my father, but never planned on telling him about me mainly because he was married with a family of his own.

I can imagine the thoughts and worries going through my mother's mind and I'd like to think that she was nervous but happy about the idea of having a little girl. I'm sure that having a child as a single woman was not always her plan. But I believe she took that with grace, knowing that she could raise a child on her own.

When I reflect on what my mother was like in her childhood through adulthood, I often wonder what the experience of accepting Christ into her heart was like. What changed in her heart? How did God speak to her? In my opinion, the person she was before Christ was so different from the person she grew to be after Christ. She didn't grow up following God or attending church regularly. But at her core, she had the greatest heart and the most vibrant spirit. Neither of those characteristics changed when she came to Christ; they grew brighter and fuller. With Christ in her life, her heart overflowed for Him and in thanksgiving to Him; and her spirit was so full of laughter and joy because of Him. Now her life as well was so much better because of Christ.

3 HELLO CANCER

Our story picks back up in the spring of 2004, three months after my mother had accepted Christ into her life. It was the last week of school, and we were walking down the steps outside of my school, Hillcrest Elementary. My mother had just picked me up from the after-school program. She pulled me aside before we got in the car, and said she had something hard to tell me. I don't remember her exact words, but I think she just blurted it out. She took my hands, looked me in the eyes, and said she was really sick with this disease called cancer, liver cancer.

There's no way a ten-year-old can fully comprehend that her mother has cancer. Not at first anyway. I remember the shock, the kind that knocks the wind out of you and takes your breath away. It's unbelievable. In a sense I understood what had just happened, but I couldn't comprehend why it was happening to us, and what this meant for our lives now.

After she told me, we went in her car and drove to Winter Park Towers, so that she could tell her boss and fellow coworkers that she had cancer. Afterwards, we walked back to the car and my mother called her older sister, Shirley. She cried a lot, talking about how she was probably going to lose her job. I was in the backseat, still in a daze. But that was the first time I had truly processed that my life as I knew it would never be the same again. That my mother was sick, so sick that soon she wouldn't be able to work. I understood fully in that car, while she was sobbing on the phone in the front seat, that my mother had a very serious disease, one that would likely kill her. And in that moment, I broke down as well.

The Rollercoaster of 2004

Once my mother was diagnosed with cancer, everything seemed to go downhill from there. Bit by bit the life we knew was being stripped away from us. My mother lost her job shortly after she was diagnosed, which meant that soon we would lose more and more of our lifestyle. Having no job, meant having no money, which meant filing for unemployment and disability. Everything seemed to have changed for us overnight; and as a young child, it was hard to come to terms with the fact that so many aspects of our lives would never be the same again.

Life at home in the beginning of my mother's cancer journey was stressful to say the least. Sometimes at home, I'd get really worried about her. Actually, it was all of the time. When she'd talk on the phone with people, I'd try to listen in so that I could get as much information from her as I could. I always worried that she was trying to hide stuff from me so I wouldn't worry about her even more than I already was. There was so much I didn't understand about what was going on. But my mother was always patient with me when I'd ask her questions about her cancer. It gave me some comfort, if only a little, to know as much as I could about what was going on.

Every time she got back from the hospital after her chemotherapy and radiation treatments, I always wanted to know what the doctors had said to her. I needed to know if she was doing better or worse, if I needed to look out for anything to take care of, or if she needed help with anything. I felt helpless so much of the time because I wanted to help her; but I knew that because I was only a kid, I couldn't always help her or make her better. My mother was always thoughtful, considerate, and patient with me when she could see that I wanted to do more for her. I could tell it was hard for her, but she always let me into this scary and confusing part of her life. She would explain things and talk with me softly, with so much love, just so I could feel better.

Even though chemo treatments, especially early on, took a lot out of her, we had some good times at home together. Since she couldn't work anymore, she had more time to spend with me. We'd watch movies and shows together, play board games and card games, and just laugh together. When she wasn't getting treatments that had her at the hospital for days at a time, we'd spend all our free time together. One of our favorite activities to do on a Friday night was going to Marble Slab Creamery and getting milkshakes to share.

Another activity that I enjoyed, and that helped relieve some of the stress I didn't realize I had, was being on the swim team at the Downtown YMCA. Swimming had always been my favorite, but I cherished moments in the pool even more after my mother was sick. There was something immediately calming about jumping into the pool and feeling like you were the only one in the water. Everything else would melt away, all my worries, frustrations, anxieties, and fears. They all disappeared as soon as my body hit the water and started moving. My only focus was on reaching the end of the pool before I'd make another lap, counting my reps. And if I was just swimming for fun, when my team didn't have practice, I could talk to God about life while I was swimming laps; just praying and laying it all out for Him while the water and I became one. Every moment I was in the water, I felt like a fish moving in synchronicity with the water. It was the best, most freeing feeling in the world.

The nights at home were harder for me though. We'd say our prayers and my mother would sing her "Goodnight" song to me.

"I want you to have a good night. Sleep tight. Love you with all my heart. If there's anything you need, let me know. Otherwise, I'll see you in the morning. Kisses. (One on each cheek) Good night."

But since my mother had started her rounds of chemo, I didn't sleep well at all. Any little sound that came from my mother's room woke me up. Some nights, I would wait a whole hour, listening for any sound that indicated that she wasn't okay before I let myself go to sleep. Common side effects of chemo and radiation are nausea and vomiting, because though these treatments are killing cancerous cells, they are also killing healthy cells at the same time. So, every time my mother would get sick and throw up, I'd get scared and hide in my room. I hated that her body was losing control and was fighting so much sickness. I especially hated that there wasn't anything I could do to make her feel better. It was hard to deal with this new reality in front of me.

With it being just her and I at home, she knew how to look out for her own body and could understand what each symptom and change meant. I didn't have to know and try to anticipate every change in her body because she was always keeping track. But that didn't mean that I didn't still worry about her immensely.

Whenever my mother was having a particularly rough day, I'd be able to stay home from school. I could always tell when she was stressed, or sad, or overwhelmed. She didn't have to explain anything to me. I just wanted to be with her all the time, for however long I could; just sitting on the couch, and listening to her heartbeat, with her soft arms wrapped around me. We were best friends from the start, and that bond deepened even more after she was diagnosed with cancer.

When her doctors first told her that she had liver cancer, my mother started writing again in journals. She'd always been an avid writer since she was young. So, it was natural for her to write down everything she was going through, especially to help process the gravity of such an immense life change. Most of her journals consist of detailed specifics of her cancer journey, including in depth medical terminology, her new diet, what was going on in her body, and how she was feeling about it all. Her extensive nursing background played a significant role in helping her understand her cancer.

Her first journal entry was on June 22, 2004. On this day, she wrote that in the beginning of her cancer journey she constantly had "*surreal, fantasy dreams with vivid colors*" where she was always trying to escape (which her older sister Shirley said was probably symbolizing her trying to escape the cancer). At this point in time, my mother was already receiving numerous rounds of chemo and radiation, and dreams were a normal side effect of the chemo and all the medications she was on. She believed that having dreams was the one intriguing aspect of the treatment's effect on her body and mind.

The next day, June 23, she received a blood transfusion and had more pleasant dreams. She wrote,

> "*Blood must have come from someone from exotic lands, because I dreamt I lived in a very old house and I was arranging many families trinkets, heirlooms, and furniture all over the house. The house had three kitchens and six different stoves. Family and friends from other countries came over and were cooking exotic dishes on all stoves. I was walking around tasting all the dishes as they cooked.*"

Since chemo and radiation treatments kept her at the hospital for long hours, days, or a full week at a time, I would stay with friends of ours from church or from school. Staying with friends would always take away some of the stress and worry from being away from my mother.

Not long after she started receiving treatment for her cancer, she was already thinking about who my guardian would be if she were to die. As dire and scary as this process was, she was always thinking of me to make sure I would be okay if anything were to happen to her. I was her only priority. But it was incredibly painful to have to ask her family or close friends if they would want to adopt me when she died. She wrote in her journal,

> *"This is one of the most difficult requests to make of anyone because it is a life changing event for all involved, including first and foremost my dearly beloved, precious gem Meena."*

I remember the process of trying to find the "right" guardian for me. My mother always kept me in the loop every step of the way. She really wanted me to be part of it with her, and she wanted me to be able to have a voice in who was going to raise me after she died. But this was a time in my life where I distinctly remember avoiding how I felt about everything that was going on. In my head I knew that this process meant that my mother would not live forever. Even if she went into remission (when the symptoms of cancer go away for a period of time), that didn't guarantee that she would even survive the cancer. I don't even think I knew what stage of cancer she had, but she was always honest with me about how bad it was.

My mother asked every close family member she could think of if they would want to take care of me, but one by one my family members all fell through. It was surprisingly hurtful; it felt like they didn't want me at all. And of course, I knew that wasn't the case. It's not that they didn't want me, it's that they couldn't take care of me the way that I needed. Even asking my mentors and friends from church didn't work out. Everyone knew they couldn't give me the life that would be best for me.

It was really hard to come to terms with the fact that I needed to find a guardian because my mother would no longer be here. I recall thinking about that and having that sinking feeling in the pit of my stomach. But I always pushed it away because I knew that wouldn't help things. My mother would worry if she knew how I felt and so I would tell myself, *'Life still goes on."* I had to help her in any way that I could while she was still there. This might have been the first time that I had those thoughts, thinking that avoiding how I was feeling was the right choice and that my feelings, thoughts, and worries were more of a burden to others. It wouldn't help to tell people how much I was suffering and scared. So, I held it in.

In the midst of searching for a guardian, my mother was still receiving chemo and radiation treatments, so she had to start wearing a port on her chest, which is a device that makes it easier for her to receive the chemo drugs. I remember how nervous and embarrassed she was to have it so visible on her chest, a noticeable bump right above her heart. She handled it though, as she handled everything, with grace and strength. But I know inside she hated it. It was another symbol of everything she had lost due to the cancer. She felt like she was losing the seemingly simple, but vital, beauties of being a woman. She had lost her hair, lost so much weight, and now had to wear an off-putting device right under her clavicle. I remember how sad she was when she had to start looking for wigs and scarves to wear too. In a journal entry from July 7, 2004, she wrote that her hair was beginning to fall out. *"More and more each day"*. She tried to hide her sadness from me, but I know how hard it was for her to accept that the cancer was taking over her more and more of her life.

Some things that calmed her were watching the night sky, the lightning from a storm, the moon, and the clouds, and listening to the birds sing. Treatment always exhausted her; it was so much extra stress on her body. Sometimes she'd get in a funk, have trouble sleeping, and have no motivation to do any activities. She'd feel extremely down especially on those days, so finding joy in the little things in life was so important for her recovery.

Going to church was also an exhausting effort, but she always felt better afterwards. Being surrounded by family and friends, and being prayed over, gave us both a lot of relief. The pastor's family, affectionately called the Rivera's, became like family to us and I made fast friends with the sisters I had first met at Vacation Bible School the previous summer. Their dad, Pastor Orlando, treated me like one of his own kids, and always called me his and Nancy's adopted daughter. My mother was always so incredibly thankful for the Rivera family and how selfless and loving they were. She called them, *"A true blessing and beautiful example of a church family loving on their community."*

In mid-October we finally had good news, my mother finished her round of chemo and radiation treatments and found out that she was in remission! No signs or symptoms of cancer! We had hopes that the cancer wouldn't spread, but knew we weren't out of the woods yet. Realistic but hopeful, we did our best to remain positive for however long her body chose to remain symptom-free.

New Home, New Fears

Behind the scenes of all the highs and lows of cancer, money remained tight for my mother and I and before we knew it, we couldn't afford to stay in our beautiful pink house any longer. When we got the news that we were being evicted from our house, my mother was devastated. In her journal she wrote,

> *"Don't want to think about it. When I was singing the "Goodnight song" to Meena, I cried a little and told her I always wanted her life to be perfect. She gently reminded me that she never expected her life to be perfect. And she mentioned God, which reminded me that this is God's plan and maybe he has bigger and better things planned for both of us. Amazing how the little ones can be strong when we need them! I love Meena so much; she is my precious gem and gift from God"*

So, in November of 2004, we moved to an apartment just a few blocks from our old house. This season was really hard for both of us. We loved our pink house, and it was crushing to know that we couldn't afford to stay there anymore. Our new home was a small apartment, but we made the most of it and chose to embrace the space we had. There aren't many memories of our time in that apartment since my mother and I often spent most of our time elsewhere. Whether it was church, the Rivera's house, or the hospital, we never seemed to be home in those days. The most prominent memory I do have of that home happened a few weeks after we were getting settled in.

One night in late November, I remember my mother and I had just finished watching a movie together and we were getting ready for bed. She came up to me in my room, stood at my door, and said to me, *"Meena, if I make a wheezing sound, like this* (proceeds to make a deep but soft wheezing sound in her throat with a small cry), *don't be scared. Come to my room and check*

19

on me, then call 911." I was already scared because my mother had never warned me about something like that before. So, we did our goodnight routine, and I went to bed, kind of waiting for what she had just described, to happen.

An hour probably went by and then I heard it. It was kind of faint, so I wasn't sure at first. But as I got out of my bed and crept to my mother's room and pressed my ear to the door, I heard her wheezing just like she described. My heart started beating faster and faster, feeling like it was beating right out of my chest, and I slowly opened the door to check on my mother. To this day, I'll never forget what I saw.

My mother was shaking violently, completely out of control of her own body. She was wheezing and her breathing was staggered, like short but quick breaths that she couldn't catch each time she tried to breathe in and out. I could only see the white of her eyes, which terrified me the most. In my head I thought, *"This isn't my mother. Something's happened to her."* Her head was jerking so violently I was sure she was going to break her neck. And I didn't realize it at the time, but she had almost bitten a hole through her tongue, so all the blood I was seeing near her head was coming from her mouth.

My heart was beating rapidly, so loud I could hear it clearly outside of my head. As I ran from her room, screaming, sobbing, and hyperventilating, I went to go find our landline phone. When I found it in the living room, it didn't have a dial tone so I couldn't even call 911. Freaking out, I ran out of the house and went over to our landlord's apartment, in the building next door. I banged on his door as hard as I could and called his name a few times until he opened the door. I don't remember exactly what I told him about what was happening, because I didn't understand it completely myself. But he knew enough to know it was an emergency, so he called 911 for me, and then we went back to my apartment.

When our landlord came inside my apartment, I remember being adamant that I didn't want to go in the house. I was too scared. He assured me that it was okay, that he had to check on my mother to make sure she wasn't hurting herself. So, while he stayed with her in the room, I waited outside for the ambulance to come. It felt like I was waiting forever, but really only about six minutes had passed until the ambulance arrived. The seconds ticked so excruciatingly slowly for me, as I sobbed, completely terrified out of my mind, waiting to hear the sirens that would let me know help was on the way.

Once the ambulance came, the paramedics ran into her room, quickly attended to my mother, and put her on a gurney into the back of the ambulance van. Still shaking, I got in the back and went with her. When we arrived at the hospital, they admitted her from the ER. As soon as she was conscious and aware of what was going on, she called the Rivera's to come pick me up because the doctors said she had to stay at the hospital for a few days. The rest of the night was a blur, but I knew I'd never forget that night.

After she was discharged from the hospital, I was told that she had a grand mal seizure because her body hadn't been receiving the medications it needed for the three months she had been in remission. It was likely a sign that her cancer was back.

Cancer Doesn't Fight Fair

Early December of that year, my mother and Nancy took a scheduled trip to the Moffitt Cancer Center in Tampa, Florida to meet with a doctor who specialized in neuroendocrine tumors of the GI tract (which is what my mother had). Neuroendocrine tumors are an uncommon cancer type in which the neuroendocrine cells become cancerous. Neuroendocrine cells are similar to nerve cells and hormone-producing cells. They carry messages from the nervous system to the endocrine system. In response to these messages, the endocrine system makes and releases hormones that control body functions like blood pressure, heart rate, digestion, breathing, and blood sugar. When these cells begin functioning abnormally, they grow and divide faster than they should, producing tumors. Visiting the Moffitt Center allowed my mother and Nancy be able to learn more about my mother's cancer and get a second opinion on her treatment. The neuroendocrine specialist there reassured my mother that he wouldn't have treated her cancer any differently than her oncologist had. He thought the way her body was responding was the best he had ever seen.

After returning from Tampa, my mother went to visit her oncologist for a checkup and to let him know what the specialist had said. A routine PET scan (an imaging test that helps reveal how your tissues and organs are functioning) showed that the cancer had grown in her liver. This was devastating news to learn, but not a complete surprise. She wasn't in remission any longer, and the cancer was back. And the fight had only just begun.

In mid-December, my mother wrote in her journal that she was starting to feel an "altered sensation" on the left side of her body, beginning in her foot. Over the course of the next few days, the sensation began to work its way up to her left clavicle. Her neurologist was concerned, and an MRI (an imaging technique that generates images of the organs in the body) of her spine confirmed that everything was normal. But my mother knew something was off; she didn't feel like herself, and just in time for the holidays. She wasn't much in the Christmas spirit that year, which was no surprise.

This was the first Christmas holiday since she was diagnosed with cancer, and my mother was determined to not let it drag us down. Writing down what we were thankful for every day was very important to her because it was too easy for us to see only the negative all around and get discouraged by everything that had happened that year. Celebrating the holidays was hard, but we still had each other.

As one year ended and another began, my mother began 2005 with a strong desire to seek out alternative treatments that would help her fight the cancer. In the beginning of January, her symptoms were getting worse, so she and Nancy went back to Tampa to see the same neuroendocrine specialist. After more testing, they found that the tumor was growing and affecting the normal function of her organs. With these results, her doctors back in Orlando knew they had more work to do.

This was an understandably stressful time for my mother, so she sought the advice and wisdom from those in our church often. People brought her a lot of encouragement on how to pray for the cancer and what direction to go in when seeking alternative treatments. God was present with her through every moment; and she received sweet reminders of His presence through the people around her.

Her journal entry said,

"The last paragraph in the pamphlet I received was extremely beneficial. It states, 'Dealing with cancer and investigating treatment options can seem overwhelming, but it remains that it is still God who sustains and directs the believer in the battle with cancer.' 'You are my hope; O Lord God, You are my confidence from my youth. By You I have been sustained from my birth' (Psalm 71:5-6). Psalm 139:16

assures us that all the days ordained for us are written in His book. He is in control, not cancer. We can have full confidence that He is near in the battles of life, great or small. 'I will never (no never) desert you, nor will I ever forsake you' (Hebrews 13:5). May God bless you as you seek His wisdom and direction."

The following weekend my mother went back to Tampa for a procedure to fix an obstruction the tumor had caused in her abdomen. After the procedure, she got pancreatitis and wasn't able to eat for five days. She could only receive nutrients through an IV, until she could gradually return to eating and drinking more solid foods. So, she lost a lot of weight that week, the lowest it had ever been.

Soon after the procedure, my mother's specialist decided to do an MRI of her brain and they found that the cancer had metastasized to her brain. Thankfully it hadn't spread to her spine, but it was still incredibly devastating and scary to hear. When cancer reaches the brain, the symptoms of treatment are more detrimental, and the quality of life is decreased significantly. The effects of using radiation treatment to treat the cancer in her brain felt like a living nightmare for my mother. In her journal she wrote, *"I felt like Marie Antoinette riding to the guillotine every day, but by the third week it became more tolerable emotionally."* In February, more tests showed that the liver tumor was growing, and that the chemo wasn't working.

In March, my mother's sister Shirley and her nieces Donna and Lynn came to visit. But this trip was more than just about spending time catching up with family. Everyone knew how bad my mother's health was, so certain hard decisions had to be made. We all knew my mother wasn't going to live much longer, especially since the cancer had spread throughout her whole body. Preparations had to be made for me, and for her, after she would pass. In the midst of such a rough time for our family, it was still good to spend quality time with them.

In April, my mother's brain scans came back normal, which meant no cancer in the brain! The tumor in her liver had also been reduced by eighty percent! The cancer wasn't completely gone, but my mother's strength and energy were coming back. There was a lot to celebrate that spring! I graduated from elementary school in May and my mother was overjoyed that she had enough energy to be able to be there for my graduation. It meant the world to me too, that she could celebrate that special moment with me. I remember the day vividly, my mother watching me with the biggest smile on her face.

That summer, my mother and I were part of Relay for Life, an annual event my middle school hosted that honored those who have cancer and those who have survived cancer. This amazing event was so special to her and was a great chance to celebrate the fact that she was still in remission. We made a beautiful banner, and our church family decorated a tent and came out to support us. We all walked around my middle school's track with my mother a couple times. Then when it got dark, everyone lit a candle in memory of, in remembrance of, or to honor someone. So, I decorated a bag and lit a candle for my mother. We both received plaques for the event honoring our volunteer work to help organize it. It was an amazing day spent reflecting on how far we had all come in my mother's cancer journey.

During the month of June, we moved to another apartment, which was closer to my new middle school. My mother and I were much happier with this apartment; but the summer was a busy one for us, with a lot of change. Even though the cancer wasn't in her brain and her liver was doing better, my mother was still receiving chemo every three weeks.

The more that things started to change around me, and the more that we started to lose our normal way of life each day, the more I started to rebel. I was so embarrassed by what our life had become, and I was growing more stressed by all of the overwhelming change and by our new lifestyle. The only way that I could make sense out of what was going on around me, was to try to provide for my own wants and "fix" the poor lifestyle I was currently living in. So, stealing seemed like the right answer to fix *some* of my problems.

At this point, we were just scraping by financially. Stealing was my way of trying to control a world that was crumbling all around me. I remember feeling like everything was being taken away from me. So, I rationalized my actions by telling myself that since my mother was sick and couldn't provide for me anymore, I could provide my own security and comfort. I always regretted my actions and apologized to the store owners and friends that I stole from. But it became harder to stop stealing and lying to those around me.

So, before long, my mother found a Christian counselor for me to see on a regular basis. She knew that I needed to work through my grief and stealing habits. I felt really comfortable talking through my stress and recurrent sin with this counselor. Early on in our sessions, she shared that she had lost her mother to cancer years before, which made it easier for me to relate to her, knowing that she could understand what I was going through.

We did a lot of practical and hands-on sessions together. During one session, we met at my house, and she brought some phone books with her. She told me that I had a lot of pent-up anger inside of me that I needed to get out. So, she encouraged me to take a phone book, rip out the pages, and tear them into small pieces. I remember how freeing it felt to rip the pieces up over and over again; getting out all of my frustration, anger, sadness, and feelings of hopelessness and defeat out on those pages. My counselor encouraged me to do that exercise whenever I felt overwhelmed and angry with life. I didn't realize I had so much anger inside of me at the time; so, through counseling, I was able to understand why I was acting out so often.

In the beginning of my mother's cancer diagnosis and treatments, I was so angry all the time. Angry at the world, at God, at my mother, and at myself. Talking it through with my counselor helped quite a bit. But I was also really scared. My mother was changing right before my eyes, she was losing weight, losing her hair, and always getting sick at home. I hated everything about the cancer, and just wanted my mother back. I just wanted her to get better. But it didn't seem like she ever would. So, it made a lot of sense that I was angry.

Even when we received good news in July that my mother was in remission again, I still held a lot of anger and frustration over anything that didn't go exactly as I'd planned, or that seemed to be out of my control. My mother would notice that I'd be frustrated with the smallest issue, and then a few minutes would pass, and I'd be smiling like nothing had happened. My counselor knew I was in serious denial of the seriousness of my mother's illness; and I would tell her often that I expected my mother to live to be 100. She would tell my mother that denial was normal for a child dealing with a parent's terminal illness; at eleven years old, a child really doesn't comprehend anything beyond one year from now. So, in my mind, I knew that my mother wasn't well, but I believed that she would still be with me for a long time. My counselor was right though, I couldn't begin to understand fully that my mother would no longer be with me one day very soon.

My mother knew that day would not be far away. So, we really had to decide who I would live with after she died. I had avoided thinking about this decision because it was just too much to bear. I just wanted it to be over with, and for someone to make it for me. Little did we know that the Rivera's had been thinking about this same decision for a while. Orlando and Nancy had always seen me as one of their daughters, so they knew it was the right choice to tell my mother and I that they wanted me to be in their family if my mother were to pass away. Their kids were actually the first ones who had brought up the idea, and so everyone was on board! I was a little reluctant at first, because I was more overwhelmed with the thought of having such a large family. But it didn't take too long for me to realize that God had provided the best option possible. So, my mother and I officially decided that the Rivera's would be my guardians.

Spiraling to Find Control and Peace

In January of 2006, I was still meeting with my Christian counselor to work on my growing anxiety and outbursts of anger. Whenever something happened out of my control and I felt like I had messed up, I would have these intense thoughts of self-hatred. It was easy for me to feel like everything happening in me and my mother's lives was my fault. Even though my counselor told my mother it was okay that I was saying these things, because I was expressing myself, my mother was still pretty concerned and worried about how I was handling everything going on.

A few days later my mother wrote this journal entry,

> *"It's normal for her to be struggling with her life. Meena's life is not that good right now. Meena puts so much pressure on herself to be perfect. I should not put too much pressure on her."*

Communicating how I felt was never easy for me, so sometimes I would over-dramatize any physical pain to mask my emotional pain as best as I could. It seemed like the only way that I could express myself. My counselor was very intuitive and helpful in communicating my behavior to my mother and to myself. She really wanted me to be able to tell my mother exactly how I felt and to be able to move out of the intense denial and anger spiral that I was in. And soon, it was easier to be honest with my mother about how I was feeling.

When I had finished my time in counseling that summer, we celebrated by taking a weekend trip to the beach. My mother was feeling a little better and had a little more energy, so the trip wasn't too much of a strain for her. It was important for us to commemorate the fact that I had completed my counseling sessions. I had been seeing my counselor for a year and had come so far. I wasn't struggling with rage anymore; and I wasn't in denial over the seriousness of my mother's illness. I was in a more realistic mindset, and I wasn't anxious over the future and our circumstances. I knew my mother wasn't doing well and wouldn't live much longer. But I had the hope of Jesus living inside of me, and I knew what to do when I would get overwhelmed with everything going on. I had learned to wholeheartedly give my cares and worries to God, knowing that He would bring peace into my heart.

Free Falling Without a Parachute

In early August of 2006, my mother noticed that she was having more pain in her body, and that her attention deficit was getting worse. She thought that the radiation was still having abnormal effects on her brain. Because of the nature of her cancer and the fact that she had "mets," which are secondary brain tumors from the original tumor site, she couldn't receive any surgical intervention. Her oncologist made it pretty clear that it was time to talk with me about her life expectancy. He knew from how her body was still fighting the cancer that she likely wouldn't live for longer than a couple more years.

On August 22, her neuroendocrine specialist confirmed that the tumor had continued to progress in her brain and liver, despite the chemo treatments. The cancer was back and was spreading further throughout her body. The work my mother had received from the procedure the year before had received great results, but the cancer came back too quickly.

She wrote in detail in one of her journals, the devastating reality that the cancer would kill her, and very soon. Clinical trials wouldn't help at this point; and there were no vital drugs that would benefit her, because of the increasing number of tumors in her brain. Although it seemed like all hope was lost, my mother never gave up on researching a solution to beating her cancer. But due to the nature of her neuroendocrine tumor, she didn't have much success. What was important and tangible at this point was maintaining a healthy diet and getting plenty of rest to ease the quality of life she had remaining, since her body would begin to slowly fail her bit by bit.

After it was confirmed that the cancer was spreading quickly and all treatments weren't working anymore, my mother began looking into Hospice programs (end of life care) where the goal was to make her comfortable since she was beyond medical treatment. Soon, my mother would need more attention throughout each day, to aid with her daily activities and medical needs, because she wouldn't be able to take care of herself. Her body would become too weak as the cancer would continue to take over.

By early September, my mother was receiving in home care from VITAS, the Hospice program. Though it felt like a huge defeat, knowing that the cancer had taken over her body completely, her doctors, friends, and family encouraged her to remember that all she needed to focus on was taking care of herself and being with family.

When VITAS started taking care of my mother, we had a nurse come to our house for hours at a time, staying for the majority of the day and at night if needed. The goal was to ease her pain, and to provide her with as much comfort as they could. My mother didn't want any more blood transfusions, ventilation, respiratory care, feeding tubes, or extensive care if her condition grew worse. She was a nurse and had done enough research to know what was going on in her body, so she knew how much time she had left. When her body was done fighting, that meant God was preparing her to go home.

The first stage of hospice care entails visits one to three times a week. The next level is intended for crisis care, with eight-hour shifts. The third level is reserved for inpatient care and is necessary when it's evident that someone's condition has reached dire levels, meaning they may have only one to two weeks left to live — the last stage of end-of-life care.

In September and October, my mother seemed to go from level to level quickly. I remember a nurse visiting us, helping out with meals and taking care of the house and my mother a couple times a week for four to six hours. She would help my mother with her medications, check her vitals and her pain levels, and help her move around when she had the energy. After two to three weeks of this, the care increased. A nurse would then stay all day for about eight to ten hours helping my mother as she grew weaker and weaker, at this point she couldn't shower or get out of bed without assistance. Before I knew it, the nurse had begun staying overnight with my mother because she had to be monitored every hour.

In October, I recall knowing deep down that my mother was going to die very soon. She couldn't take care of herself at night, and it wasn't safe for her to be left on her own, so I was very thankful that a nurse was with her, constantly monitoring her. It was getting harder for me to sleep at night, because I couldn't stop worrying about her. I kept fearing that I would wake up one day and she would be gone. We would always tell each other that we loved each other at least fifty times a day, but the urgency of expressing my love for her became more of a desperate cry that she wouldn't leave me. I remember feeling like I had to spend every second telling her how much I loved her.

One day, my mother became unresponsive and went into a coma really early in the morning, hours before the sun had come up. The nurse called 911 and soon many medical EMTs and professionals came rushing into our house. Immediately they took my mother to the hospice facility where she could be comfortable. My family from Maryland flew in that day, and I stayed at their hotel with them that night after visiting with my mother. I visited her as much as I could every day after, talking to her, crying over her, praying for her, and reading her Bible to her. Shirley, Donna, and Lynn would take me back to the hotel every few hours so that I could try to nap. I was so scared that my mother would die without me being by her side, so it was really hard to get any sleep.

After midnight, on the 23rd of October 2006, I remember someone calling Shirley and telling her that my mother didn't have long left. I watched her as she got that call and immediately knew that it was time to say goodbye to my mother for the last time. So, with heavy hearts, we drove to the hospice facility, and they let me say goodbye to my dear mother. I remember sobbing as I kissed her goodbye and telling her it was okay; that I'd be okay and that she could go home to be with God. I told her that I loved her very much and that I would love her forever. I waited in the waiting room for about an hour, while a friend of my mother's waited with her as she drew her last breath. It might've been around two or three in the morning when she passed away, I can't remember when exactly, but I remember the deep breath I took when I heard that she was gone. I was crushed, but relieved that my mother wasn't in pain any longer. Shirley, Donna, and Lynn (who I had grown to fondly call my grandma and my aunts) held me as I sobbed, and then we left the facility.

The days that followed are somewhat of a blur to me. My grandma Shirley, Aunt Donna, and Aunt Lynn hung around as my mother was cremated and preparations were made for her celebration of life service. I felt like my entire life had evaporated right before my eyes, into this vast dark hole below my feet. Everything I ever knew was gone. I lived in a daze for the next couple of weeks. I hadn't cried since the night that my mother had died, but on the day of her celebration of life service, I sobbed from the core of my being the entire time. We had a beautiful service celebrating of her life that day, but it was one of the hardest days I had ever walked through.

Our cancer journey was over. My mother passed away and went home to be with the Lord on October 23rd, 2006. It was a day I'll never forget as long as I live. My life was changed forever. I had no idea how to live in a world without my mother. It didn't seem real, and I couldn't fathom what life would look like now. My mother, my best friend in the whole world, was gone. Forever.

An article from the Orlando Sentinel was written about her and the legacy she left for me. It read,

> "Darlene Dee Paes knew her time was short, but the cancer patient was determined to spend every minute possible ensuring her young daughter would be well taken care of... She recorded audio tapes, put together photo albums to chronicle their life together...". Orlando, my newly appointed legal guardian at the time, had said, *"'She (Darlene) felt at peace with God, and she had found a home for her daughter... I felt like she was sent to us to prepare to die. And once she understood she was going to die, she did everything in her power to get things in order.'"*

The next stage of my life had begun in a foreign world where my mother didn't exist anymore. All I could do was take one deep breath at a time.

PART II

4 LIFE AFTER DEATH

The days after my mother died were like passing through a foggy haze. Life seemed to move without me. I was standing still, watching everything play in fast forward, like a carousel going round and round, images and people a complete blur. I had come to realize fairly quickly, that nothing would ever be the same again.

During my mother's celebration of life service, the pews filled with family and friends seemed to permeate the church. I sat in the front with my family from Maryland and the Rivera family, barely noticing those around me. I don't remember the kind words said to me, nor the hugs and brief pats on my shoulder. I only remember sobbing for what felt like hours. Everything became too much to bear once I realized why I was in that church, why I was sitting in that pew.

At some point our pastor, Orlando, began to speak to the crowd. He picked up a piece of paper, saying words that I had written down, words that I was supposed to say about my mother but couldn't bring myself to speak aloud. We sang some songs and hymns, my mother's favorites of course, and more people spoke, sharing memories and of the legacy she had left behind.

We ended the service with a reception, and everything seemed to fade around me. I was there, but it didn't feel like I was physically there. I was trapped inside my own body, surrounded by a cloud of despair and loneliness. I made small niceties and smiled as much as I could after the service was over, but inside it was like I was barely existing. Life didn't seem to make sense anymore now that my mother was gone. Any activity, even as simple as interacting with others, took everything out of me. Just taking one step in front of the other was all I could manage.

My New Normal

After my grandma and aunts left to go spread my mother's ashes over her parents' graves back in Maryland, I moved into the Rivera family's house. Orlando and Nancy became my legal guardians, and my new life with them began. I had a large family now, three brothers, three sisters, and a new baby brother who was born the day before my mother's service. It was quite the transition from being an only child to a family with eight kids. I had grown up in a home where it was just me and my mother, but now my entire family of two had disappeared. Seemingly overnight, I became part of this large family. I had no idea what my life would look like from now on; all I knew for sure was that everything had changed.

Life at school was different too. Everyone knew what had happened to my mother. So, once I went back, it felt like my friends and classmates saw me as "the kid whose mother had died". In order to avoid having to talk about my mother, I put up this façade, acting like everything was normal, when that couldn't have been further from the truth. Smiling when I didn't feel like smiling and telling people quick answers to their questions about how I was doing became my new normal. I felt like a stranger in my own body, having to act like I was this person who was doing okay when in reality my entire life had completely fallen apart.

One bright spot about life at my new home was that I shared a room with Ashley, my close friend in the family and the sister who was only three months younger than me. We were already good friends before I moved in but became best friends and sisters very quickly. Our personalities and temperaments could not have been more opposite, but that's partly why we got along so well. We balanced each other out and had a fun time whenever we were together. I was shy; she was outgoing. I was quiet; she was loud. I was neat; she was messy. I was a pushover; she was stubborn and a fighter. I held my feelings in; she said exactly what she was feeling. The list goes on. But every second with her was full of adventure. She helped me learn all about the world beyond my sheltered view and brought me out of my shell to explore that world. She introduced me to all kinds of music, and we found similarities in what we loved to sing and blare in our room. She helped me walk through puberty and my first middle school crush. She helped bridge the gap when it felt too awkward or weird to talk to my new parents. We talked and laughed about everything together. Seeing her as my sister was the easiest part of transitioning into the family.

I observed all of my siblings a lot in that first year, just trying to learn how the family operated to see how I fit with them. I wanted to feel like a part of the family, but it took some time. I felt like the outsider who had awkwardly fallen into the family rhythms, not at all sure how I belonged and out of the loop with their inside jokes and traditions.

I kept how I felt about my new family carefully hidden away in my mind; I never thought to tell them any of it. It didn't feel polite or okay to share with them, because they had given me so much in opening their home and their family to me. My reluctance to share how I was feeling led to an even deeper avoidance of telling anyone how I felt about my grief and loss. I pushed those feelings so far down that even if I tried to process how I was doing, I would've been at a complete loss.

The Black Hole of Initial Grief

The concept of grief was so foreign to me and, seemingly, was also foreign to those around me. My siblings never asked me much about how I was doing. Orlando and Nancy always checked in whenever they could, but I couldn't even verbalize what was going on inside, and I didn't want to try. While everyone tried to find the right words to say and tried to help me the best way they knew how, I was numb inside. I didn't want to let myself feel all the emotions raging within me.

But as soon as that dam broke, grief came flooding in. During the quiet lonely hours of the night, I came to learn that everything I had felt the night my mother drew her last breath and how broken I felt the day of my mother's service, were more than I could handle. The grief of realizing that I had lost my best friend, and that she was never coming back, was overwhelming, I felt like I was drowning over and over again. Feeling the intensity of those emotions even for a minute was too painful to experience. It was like the depth of my own feelings shocked me, leaving me literally without breath. If I even thought about it for a second, I felt trapped in my own body. I couldn't think, breathe, or move because the pain was so real and intense.

Instead of letting myself process all of that grief, I chose to bury how I felt. I feared that if I let myself feel everything all at once, that I wouldn't make it. I wouldn't survive that kind of pain. Most of each day, just existing and knowing that my mother was gone, that I'd never get to talk to her, or hug her, or tell her that I loved her again, was painful enough.

Any second that I had a moment to myself, I further retreated into the black hole that existed in my mind. A thought would slip through, and I'd remember that my mother had died, and this sharp intense pain would form in my chest, looking down I knew that the pain was coming from my heart. It would hurt so much that I couldn't seem to breathe or even move. As soon as I'd feel that depth of sadness pierce through, I would force myself to move on to something, anything, that could distract me from my feelings.

School became my main distraction, and so I relied on my homework and school projects to take me away from thinking about my mother and her death. I consistently chose to avoid thinking about how I felt, because it hurt too much. I didn't want to talk about it or think about it at all. Every day after I got home from school, I'd jump right into doing my homework until it was dinnertime. Any free moment after that was spent reading from my growing stack of library books.

Most of the time, I would distract myself with a book for hours and hours. It was the perfect way to fade into another reality, where I could live in a different world and embark on a mysterious journey with each story. That way I wouldn't have to think about loss at all. I wouldn't be stuck thinking about my mother and about how much I missed her and how I wished she was there with me. I wasn't about to give myself any time to let my mind wander.

The moments that lasted a little longer, when there wasn't an easy distraction nearby, I'd ponder saying something to someone. To Orlando or Nancy, or to Ashley. But I'd look over at one of them, see them busy doing something or talking to someone, and I'd put those feelings away. Telling myself, *"Oh, they don't have time. They wouldn't want to hear about this. I'm not going to worry them about it. It's okay. It doesn't matter. They wouldn't understand and I don't want to make them feel awkward trying to find the right words to say. It's fine. I'll be fine."* Any variation of that mantra would run through my mind each time I considered talking about my grief. I didn't understand what I was feeling almost every day, so how could anyone else?

Even on the days when I could put words to how I was feeling that I just missed my mother, it felt wrong to say that out loud to them. It felt like I wasn't grateful to them for opening their hearts and their home to me, like they weren't good enough. Soon I would have to start calling Orlando "Dad" and Nancy "Mom", and I wasn't ready for that yet. So, to tell them that I missed my mother so much that it physically hurt my heart, just seemed cruel. It made more sense to hold it inside. I thought my pain was manageable, and I didn't want to cause them pain after they had given me so much. So subconsciously, I pushed the pain of grief down even more.

Forever Knit in the Family Fold

But I couldn't hide how much pain I was in for very long. Orlando could always tell when I was feeling down. I wouldn't have to say a word, and he'd know that I wasn't okay. He'd talk with me and ask me how I was, letting me share however much I wanted. I would keep it brief at first, until during one of our talks I just knew that he was someone I could trust. He was a person so attuned to the Holy Spirit that he always knew exactly how I was feeling, especially when I couldn't express it myself. He'd ask me questions that prompted responses I didn't realize I needed to process through. He'd pray with me earnestly, intentionally, and deeply; and he wasn't put off by my emotions and tears, he welcomed them. I felt safe to express how I was truly feeling at any given moment, knowing that he actually cared for me and loved me as one of his daughters.

In the beginning, I had always felt like a random and unplanned addition to the family. But Orlando made me feel like I was at home with them. He treated me like I was part of his family, even before I knew I would become part of his family. Orlando knew that it was always in God's plan for me to be his daughter. The same as he felt about each and every one of his children, adopted and biological, bore no difference to him. We were all his children, no matter how we came to be part of the family. So, in all of our talks, I would be honest with him about how I felt; and afterwards, the pain in my heart would lessen a little bit each time.

5 SIGNIFICANT DAYS

As soon as I got used to having a large family and feeling like I was one of the Rivera's, grief decided to rear its dark head again. Most of the summer during that year had been spent hanging out with my new family and traveling to visit extended family. But it also meant my mother's birthday was coming up in August, and I would be spending it without her for the first time. This was the first significant holiday where I actually considered letting myself feel the full intensity of my grief, because I couldn't avoid thinking about her and missing her anymore. Not on her birthday. My mother and I loved celebrating birthdays. So, I couldn't numb my feelings for this one.

Since my mother died in October of that previous year, I had celebrated Thanksgiving, Christmas, and my birthday without her. The holidays had passed by, leaving me void of feeling. I can't even recall how I spent those days or how I felt attempting to celebrate. I had forced myself to not think about my mother for so long, that by the time the holidays were rolling around, I was too angry to be happy. If my mother wasn't there to celebrate the season with me, then I wouldn't celebrate at all. But for her birthday, I knew I had to let myself remember her.

A couple weeks before my mother's birthday, I decided that I wanted to be left completely alone so I could remember and miss her in my own way. The only things I had left of my mother shortly after she passed were our family photo albums, and some small mementos like her jewelry and picture frames of her and I that I displayed in my room. One day I shut myself in my room for hours and just poured through the albums and mementos. Looking at her pictures and the good times we had shared, every part of my being was consumed with missing and mourning my mother.

Once August 4th came around, my mother's first birthday in heaven, I had a lot of pent-up anger and sorrow buried deep inside. This was the first birthday of hers that I was spending without her with no card to write her and no way to show her how much I loved her, no hugs, no kisses, nothing. As this reality came crashing in around me, everything that was pent up inside came rushing out. The grief came flooding back and all the walls I had put up around my heart were torn down. I couldn't stop the tears and the sobs that shook my body to its core. I felt torn between wanting to avoid feeling everything and wanting to remember my mother because I missed her so much. I felt like I owed it to her to remember her, especially on her birthday. No matter how much it pained me on the inside.

So, I took a deep breath, and remembered as much as I could. Memories came flooding back in, her smell, her touch, her voice, her words, her overwhelming and all-consuming love. I let myself miss her, and I let my thoughts run wild where I wished she was with me. I let myself imagine a different future, where she hadn't died, and I let myself feel every ounce of pain, knowing a different future was not my reality. My sorrow enveloped every part of me. I was broken down, devastated, and angry. And that's all I felt. There was no hope, no joy, no "moving on." I sat in the depth of my despair and reality, with no hope of getting out.

Prolonged Grief

What I didn't expect was that the grief-turned despair continued to stick with me for the rest of the month. I was in severe emotional pain for weeks, grieving in my own way. It was like I had entered this other world. I felt absent from the real world because all that consumed my entire being was sadness and longing. The longing for my mother left me trapped in a deep, dark chasm of my mind. I'd go on and on thinking of how much I wished she was there with me. How much I missed her. How much I wished she was there to talk to. How much I hated that she wasn't there. How much I hated the cancer and hated that she had to die. In this chasm, I existed solely to let the anger and feelings of agony in my heart run wild.

Outwardly, I felt actual pain in my chest. My heart ached for my mother, and I would feel sharp pain followed by a prolonged burning in my heart. When it became evident that the pain wasn't going to end anytime soon, I would be racked with heaving sobs that came from a place I didn't know existed within me. I would cry and cry for hours alone in my room. Unable to console myself and unwilling to let others console me, I felt like I was dying, and I wanted to die. I didn't want to live in a world where my mother didn't exist. I wanted desperately to be with her in Heaven.

Eventually I got to the point in my grief where the emotional and physical pain was too much, and I couldn't see how I could be happy while thinking of my mother. I couldn't let myself wallow in sorrow and grief forever because it was making me feel completely miserable. I told myself that I needed to bury my grief again. I needed to actualize the fact that life still went on even though my mother was gone. I still had to face the real world and school. I couldn't be sad around other people, or they'd ask me about it; and there was no way that I was going to talk to anybody about how I was feeling. Anytime I could tell that the grief was threatening to overwhelm me, I'd get angry with myself and push it down, boarding up those walls again and hiding the grief where it couldn't be found.

So, I began eighth grade, and my mother was the furthest thing from my mind. My last year of middle school was mainly spent trying to establish my new normal. I dove into whatever could keep my attention away from thinking about my mother. Daydreaming and reading were my main escapes, outside of homework and hanging out with my friends. I probably read a hundred fiction novels that year, anything to get me away from my own reality.

Heaven-anniversary

Once October 23rd came around though, I fell back into my dark hole. It was exactly one year since my mother had died. Somehow one whole year had passed, and I couldn't believe it. I don't recall doing anything significant that day, maybe I took the day off from school. But I do remember I felt the sense of impending doom since the month of October had begun. It was like I was preparing myself to be in a state of mourning for a long time. I looked through my albums and let myself feel once again. I spent a lot of time alone, shut away from everyone again. And just like around my mother's birthday, that dark state of mind stuck with me for the next few weeks.

Grief that month was like the living the part in Alice in Wonderland when she first falls into the rabbit hole. Falling slowly further and further down this dark hole until at some point, I wake up in another land. But it's not a land of fun new adventures. It's a land where all I can see and all I can feel are memories of my mother; and the questions that I'm asking subconsciously, surround me everywhere I go.

I questioned God, but not because I wanted a response. I cried out to Him, blaming Him for everything that had happened, and for how I was feeling. I questioned why my mother had to die and why He had to take her from me. I told God, *"I miss her. I wish she was here. She was my best friend, my most favorite person in the whole world. I wish I could talk to her, hug her, tell her I loved her. Did I even tell her I loved her in the end? Is she looking down at me now? Is she proud of me? I want her back. Please bring her back to me. This isn't fair. This hurts so much; it hurts too much. Where is she? Why isn't she here with me right now? Please make it stop, make the pain stop. Why does my heart have to hurt so much? I want to be with her. I don't want to be here right now."* The questions ran through my mind over and over again. I spent most of my time alone that month lying in the fetal position on the floor or on my bed, crying softly. My chest heaving up and down, wishing to be consoled, but only by my mother.

At one point in my grief, my relationship with God became strained and distant because I couldn't understand why He would take my mother from me. The only reason that made sense in my mind, was that God had taken her because I loved and valued her more than I should have, that my love put her higher in my mind than God. I knew He wanted me to see Him as the most important person in my life; but I also knew that I viewed my mother as the most important person in my life, even after her death.

This led me to believe that God was punishing me for the love I had for my mother. Even as a kid I knew this wasn't His character, but whenever I would ask Him in my prayers why she had to die, He was silent. God wouldn't answer that question. So, whenever I tried to figure out the answer on my own, I ended up blaming Him, or myself, for her death. I was so angry that God allowed her to die and leave me; and I felt abandoned by Him because He wasn't giving me the answers I needed to try and understand her loss. So, I stopped praying for a long time.

Light at the End of the Tunnel?

Grief was such a strange concept to me in that first year without my mother. The only way I understood it was through pain; to me, grief was pain. It literally broke your heart, and it shattered your life. It took the breath out of you and left you lying on the floor crying until you had no more tears or energy left. It stripped you bare, and left you empty. The grief of losing my mother felt worse than the day she died. I was left alone with the reality that she was gone forever, and that I would have to continue living life without her. That was what was unbelievable; that this person who was my whole world, was now gone from my world. I couldn't comprehend it; and any time that I tried to, I was left in so much pain that I thought I was dying from the inside.

A few weeks after my mother had passed, Orlando and Nancy gave me a workbook so that I could try to process my grief. In the back of the workbook was a letter for the owner to declare over themselves to further encourage healing and convicting truth.

It reads, *"Dear Me, Not so long ago, my world felt shattered and I didn't know how I could hold on another day. But somehow, I found the courage to believe in me, in life, and in the possibility of miracles. What I've learned has shown me the power of my heart. What I've endured has made me stronger. What I feel makes me real. And all that I love and value gives me hope to carry on. I will take the lessons I've learned and lean on them whenever times get hard. I will share my truths with others. Most of all, I will value the memory, I will hold love and life more dearly, and I will never, ever forget. No matter what, I will remember that there will always be goodness in the world, and that thinking, believing, and acting upon positive thoughts can change the course of my life. I will become all that I yearn to be, and I will let myself embrace each moment I am given, for I am the brave. Forever, Meena Paes. Signed January 1st, 2007."*

Though I struggled to believe all of these truths I had read and affirmed within myself, I knew that they were indeed true. But I wasn't ready to process anything, so I let the workbook collect dust on my bookshelf. There was no way that I could keep experiencing my grief over and over again, so I resolved to keep it locked away forever. I couldn't fathom surviving any other way. But I did take to heart what the statement said about remembering goodness and acting upon positive thoughts.

From then on, I promised myself that if anyone asked how I was doing, I would just say that I was fine or that I was okay. So, I put on a fake smile and kept my feelings inside. I needed to try to see the good in the world instead of dwelling on everything bad that had happened. The demeanor I showed everyone quickly became real, and I did begin to have a positive outlook on life.

People who were just getting to know me after that first year of mourning couldn't understand why I was so positive. I would tell them that it was all because of God, since I couldn't really understand it either. My relationship with God was still strained, but I knew He hadn't left me through it all. I was only standing because of Him, and I held onto that truth. I was blessed and felt thankful, even though from the inside my world had completely crumbled to ashes before me. The version of myself that I showed the world gradually became who I was on the inside. I found reasons to be happy and brushed aside any version of grief. My new way of life worked for me, and I truly believed that I had made the right decision to stay positive and be thankful. I felt like my season of grief was finally over.

By the time ninth grade came around, I dove into school even further. All that mattered was getting through the year and passing my classes. All in all, I felt like I was handling everything pretty well.

But in the spring, my dad, Orlando, got his dream job as a professor at Nyack College and was going to be pastoring a new church plant in Mount Vernon, New York. Life was about to change drastically once again. We would soon be leaving everyone and everything behind for a new life in the Big Apple.

6 NEW YORK, NEW YORK

The summer of 2009 we moved to Nyack, a college town in upstate New York. Our quaint new life at home was anything but; tensions were high and everyone at home struggled to adjust to the move. We had left our hometown, and our family and friends behind, so adapting to all the change was rough for everyone.

Saying goodbye to my friends wasn't even real until we were driving away. I remember sitting in the backseat of our twelve-passenger van, texting my friends, and telling them how much I would miss them and how much I promised that we would stay in touch. But as the months passed, it grew harder and harder for us to keep up with each other.

With a fresh start at a new high school, I entered tenth grade with the intention of redefining myself, to be the outgoing and funny new kid instead of the reserved kid. I wanted to set myself apart so I could seem more interesting. But at the same time, I really didn't want to make any new friends, because I was afraid those wouldn't last. I didn't want to get to know anybody, but I still wanted to be accepted. As I quickly discovered, trying to be a different version of myself wasn't as easy as I thought. So, the shy but approachable demeanor stuck around.

Since I couldn't change my personality, I decided to try and change my style and appearance so I could fit in at school. Before I knew it, I was falling into the teenage trap of wanting to be a more perfect version of myself. I looked in the mirror, but constantly hated the person I saw looking back. My insecurities had been dormant for a while, but now they were right at the surface, like an all-consuming fire. Inside I was miserable, but I told myself that was fine because I was used to feeling that way.

As time passed, that misery grew into something else entirely. I started to hate everything about my life. Hanging out at the park with my family, playing video games with my brothers, reading, and even swimming laps at swim team practice only seemed to satisfy my desire to be happy for a short period of time. Activities that should've reminded me of how good my life was, only gave me brief moments of peace and a fake smile. My happiness was constantly fleeting, and joy was non-existent. I struggled with low self-esteem, no self-confidence, self-image issues, rage, frustration, worry, and unhappiness. I wasn't concerned though; I figured all teenagers dealt with that.

But the more I thought about it, the more I began to realize that it wasn't a good thing that my happiness was short lived and forced ninety percent of the time. And maybe my increasingly negative perspective on life wasn't okay either. Something was wrong, and I needed to find a way to fix myself in order to feel better.

Even though I hated the person I had become, I realized that somehow other people felt differently. I had tried to avoid making friends, but despite my reluctancy in the beginning, I still managed to make some anyway. They appreciated and enjoyed the person I already was, and actually wanted to spend time with me. I had hoped that having friends would solve everything and make me happy again. But instead, some new insecurities arose.

The Storm of Emotional Turmoil

I hadn't planned to have feelings for anyone in high school, but over the course of my tenth and eleventh grade years, I fell in love (at least I thought I did) with a friend. I was convinced he didn't feel anything towards me, until at some point, the friendship grew into something more. Our time together was spent in secret and in sin; and though I knew it was wrong, I wanted to feel seen and appreciated by someone. So, I kept the secret and willingly lived in the shame of falling into temptation over and over again, for fear of losing our friendship completely. But soon, the shame, embarrassment, and constant heartache ate away at me. During our "relationship", and even after it ended when he moved away, my self-loathing spiraled and every emotion I felt inside was stained black. I hated myself more than I thought possible, and I had no way of dealing with it except internally, because telling those around me what was going on never felt like an option.

As a teenager, I had no concept of what depression was, or what it meant to be in emotional distress. I thought dealing with life meant living in sadness and in pain, at least for me. Hurt and pain was hurt and pain, and that was it. Since my mother had died, almost three years ago at this point, I had gotten very good at avoiding how I was really feeling. Pushing down my feelings was like second nature to me. But something was different about it this time. Now I had to admit how I was feeling. I couldn't live in denial anymore. I had to acknowledge how I felt and give my emotions the attention they deserved. I needed to be honest with myself and I needed to stop hiding behind any and every distraction I could find.

My heartache wasn't going anywhere, and the regret and shame I felt about how I had acted and deceived my family and friends was constantly on my mind. I couldn't avoid how much pain I was in even if I tried. It was all impossible to bury, and I knew I had to give in to the pain. Nothing could relieve my heart from its suffering, but I knew I wasn't about to tell anyone what was going on inside. It was mortifying to be this devastated over a boy. I knew I had sinned over and over again, but I couldn't fathom confessing my embarrassment and pain with anyone. I felt like I had no way out from my agony; so, I just lived in it and let it consume my entire being. Before I knew what was happening, my grief erupted and latched itself onto my heartbreak and onto every insecurity I had.

I think what set me over the edge and into emotional turmoil, was that I didn't have anyone to confide in. I would in no way have ever told my parents or any of my siblings about the "relationship." The one person I wanted to talk to about it wasn't there. My mother. It was in the quiet moments alone in my room where I began to think about her again; to allow myself to miss her and wonder what she would have said to me, what advice she would have given. So, I would talk to her in my mind and have conversations where I explained to her how I was feeling. But in doing that, the grief would slowly seep in as well.

Grief this time sucked me into a vortex of despair and longing for my mother. I was trapped in this intense storm of grief, where despair and longing became part of me. I desperately desired to be loved by someone and longed for my affections to be returned. But I also desired for my mother to be with me and longed for her love and companionship to return. It felt like sheer agony. And now I couldn't turn it off. Because as soon as my thoughts lingered on the "relationship", I also thought about how much I wished my mother was still with me.

I began to dream about her too; real visceral dreams where my reality was different. In my dreams she hadn't died, and different scenarios would emerge where the reason for her absence was made clear. She had been away on a long trip and was now back home. Or she had been in witness protection for some vague and mysterious reason. The reasons were different in every dream; but in each one we had a new life now that she was back. We could talk all the time and we lived in extravagant homes, and all was right in the world. In my dream state of being, we were blissfully happy.

When I would wake up from these painfully real dreams, having just lived out my deepest desire where my mother is back in my life, the agony would set in again. I would sit up in bed, relive the dream, and quickly brush it all aside, because a new day was beginning where I would have to come to terms with other painful realities. Not only was my mother not alive, but the heartbreak and shame were still there. No matter how I felt inside, life had to continue as normal, like nothing was wrong. This double lifestyle I was living, where how I felt inside was so vastly different from the person I presented myself to be on the outside, grew increasingly exhausting.

Reaching the End of My Rope

***The following pages contain sensitive and possibly triggering details about depression and suicide. Stop and care for yourself before reading this next section of my story. ***

I honestly don't recall the first time it happened. But for many months during the year we lived in Nyack, New York, I reached a breaking point, and my hidden feelings of agony, despair, longing, and shame became too much to bear. I couldn't comprehend why my mind was so at war with itself. I had become someone I didn't recognize. I was so angry and sad all the time. My anger and sadness didn't feel like emotions anymore but had blended into this constant state of being. It was like I didn't have "emotions" anymore. I was nothing and felt nothing. The agony I was living in turned numb. Many nights I would get so angry at myself for not feeling anything inside, that I desperately sought to feel something on the outside. So, I began cutting.

I didn't do it to bring any lasting pain, but because I desperately wanted to get out of my own miserable head. It started with just digging my fingernails into my palms or my forearms, but then it grew into taking any sharp object and digging it into my skin. I wanted to hurt just enough so I could feel some lasting external pain, but I never wanted to draw actual blood. Cutting seemed to stop the dull numbness that filled my entire being. No one knew and it didn't seem like a problem because I had it under control, at least that's what I kept telling myself.

For some reason, I still felt invisible, alone, and numb most of the time. I felt unloved and undesired, a waste of a person. I didn't like who I saw in the mirror, this stranger I had become. While my friends were going out and starting to have real relationships, I knew the guy I had fallen for wasn't going to pursue me the honorable way; and our secret "relationship" left me feeling less cared about than I had ever felt before. So, the cutting happened more often every night when no one was around to notice. Giving myself parameters for my self-harm helped me feel responsible and in control of my own pain, therefore making it okay in my mind.

But something happened one night that sent me over the edge. I'm not sure exactly what it was, but for the first time I wanted to cut myself enough to bleed. I wanted to leave more than a mark, but it was too hard to make myself go further. I wanted to have the willpower to cut deeper, but I didn't. I can't remember who, but one of my sisters noticed my wrists and tried to talk to me about it. I don't remember our conversation, but seeing her concern and worry opened my eyes for the first time. I started to realize that what I was doing was wrong, and that I needed to stop before it got worse. I'm so thankful she noticed because that night was the last time I cut myself.

Making the decision to stop cutting didn't instantly change how I felt about myself or my life. I was still hopelessly upset that my life wasn't in any way how I wanted it to be. My mother was dead, I had engaged in a sinful relationship with a friend, I felt invisible at home, and now someone noticed my scars. I was so ashamed and embarrassed. I couldn't even bear to look at myself.

I was in such a dark place that I knew without a doubt I didn't want to feel anything at all, but I didn't want to feel numb either. I didn't want to exist. I wanted to die. I felt like no one would care if I was gone because I certainly didn't anymore. My world seemed to be crumbling around me and I felt so alone. It seemed like even if I told someone, no one would understand what I was going through or how I was feeling. I still wasn't going to tell my parents, because I was too embarrassed and ashamed that it had gotten to this point.

So, I talked to God about whether it was okay to want to die or not, if killing myself was a sin or not. I wanted to die, but I wanted to leave this earth and know whether I would go to Heaven or not. Many nights I prayed about suicide and read through the Bible to see if it was a sin; if I could still go to Heaven if I killed myself. At this point, my relationship with God was very surface level. I listened to sermons and prayed before each meal, but that was it. I didn't understand the concept of my salvation fully, but I knew that I needed to honestly pray and talk to God about how I was feeling. Discussing suicide with Him was the only way I could come to terms with debating the finality of my life and my overwhelming depression. I had lost purpose and saw no worth in my life at all. So why continue living?

After many discussions with God on many dark nights, I came to my own conclusion that killing myself would be a sin. I compared it to committing murder, to myself. I would be killing someone and even though that person was me, that didn't make it any less okay. How could I do that to someone God cared about? How could I do that to the people on earth who did care about me? I needed to take the dilemma and think of it outside of myself. I didn't care about myself, but knowing that other people very likely did, and that God definitely did, caused me to think about how they would feel if I died. I didn't know for sure what my eternity would look like if I killed myself, but I imagined God watching me do it. It broke my heart to think about how painful it would be to watch someone you love commit suicide. I couldn't do that to God or to anyone else.

But coming to that conclusion and deciding not to kill myself still didn't change how I felt on the inside yet. I still didn't love who God had created me to be. I knew in my heart that I didn't love myself. And I knew that God didn't want that for me, just as much as He didn't want me to hurt His daughter by ending her life. He gently reminded me that He loved me. Though I didn't love myself, His love for me would be enough. He knew that one day I would be able to love myself too. I read about God's love in the Bible and knew that I desired that. Desired to understand what it meant to love myself.

I was still in a dark place, and I didn't know how to feel genuinely happy about anything. But I didn't want to die anymore. I wanted to learn how to live again.

It's been interesting to go back and relive the memories from a time where depression and suicide were very real to me. I can recall many moments where I didn't see the point in living. I didn't think my life had meaning anymore. I had gotten to the point where I looked at where I was in my life and didn't see anything worth sticking around for. The pain of living in those moments became too real. So, the only solution and the only thoughts running through my mind, were that I should end it all. That I should end my life and then everything would be fine.

As I was writing this section, I spent many months thinking a lot about my younger self. She buried so much pain inside, and I want to tell her that the pain will not last forever but will be used for good.

> *Your life is not over. Your worth is not futile. Your value is not fragile or useless. Your life is not over. There is more than this. People can do better and not everyone will hurt you. There are people who will love you deeply for who you are. Don't give up. Keep holding on. I'm so sorry. You are not alone.*

I've also come to realize that even when I didn't see it, God was there every step of the way. He never gave me more than I could handle, even when it felt like I couldn't go on any longer. He was there alongside me, telling me and showing me everything I had to live for.

Even though my relationship with God was rocky at times, I knew He was there with me, even on my darkest of days. I knew to cry out to Him in my deepest moments of despair, even when everything seemed to be crashing down all around me and when I felt so lost. God saved me in many ways back then, even though I couldn't fully understand why I was feeling the way I was. He never gave up on me even when I was giving up on myself. He knew that my story wasn't over, even though I thought it was.

I really thought my life was over and that there was nothing left for me on this earth, but God helped hold on. The night I decided to stop cutting, God gave me hope. He gave me a desire to not give up on myself, to keep questioning Him, and to discover what His love for me actually meant. God did so much more for me on those nights I talked to Him about suicide than I'll ever comprehend. I am eternally grateful that my life is not my own, and that God is faithful to redeem and restore us no matter how lost we are.

7 AN UNWELCOME REALITY CHECK

The summer before I started eleventh grade, we moved to Mount Vernon, New York to be closer to the church plant my dad was pastoring. We left behind some friends, so I resolved once again to avoid making new ones. I didn't have a lot of hope that this year, going to another new high school, would be any better than the last. Honestly, I didn't want to think about the previous year at all.

I had let God into my pain and heartbreak, but there was no flip of the switch. I didn't wake up each day loving myself the way God loved me. My depression, and the growing temptation to continue rebelling against my parents, overcame my desire to live the way God called me to. I kept looking for love in all the wrong places (by still entertaining the secret relationship) and struggled to admit to myself where I had fallen short and hurt those around me. I wanted to understand God's love for me and live the way He was calling me live (by repenting and turning away from habitual sin), but I didn't want to give up how I chose to live my life (accepting of habitual sin). I thought happiness was a far-fetched idea; so, I told myself that I was happy enough with the illusion of love from others. Therefore, everything I did became like an artificial band aid, only temporarily keeping the pain of my own reality from bleeding out.

My self-esteem, self-confidence, and self-worth were lower than ever. I talked down to myself constantly, had a terrible self-image, and was desperate for affirmation and affection from those around me. So, at school it became normal and acceptable for me to be objectified and teased for my looks; many other girls were treated the same, so I didn't think anything of it. I wanted to be accepted and valued, so I took those crude comments as compliments and affirmations. But I grew to hate the person I had become and was tired of living a life of shame and regret every day. The last thing I wanted to do was look inward and evaluate where my life had gone wrong, but that's exactly what I needed to do.

During Sunday mornings at church, it wasn't easy for me to avoid the shame and regret I felt because of how I had been living my life. But every week my dad's sermons became more and more convicting. I would feel this nagging feeling, urging me to admit that I needed to change. I was deeply convicted that I shouldn't have been seeking affirmation and love from a relationship hidden in secret sin. Even though that "relationship" ended later that fall because my friend moved away, I deeply regretted that I had let it go on for so long.

It took some time before feeling convicted didn't immediately lead me to judge myself harshly. I regretted everything about the relationship I had kept hidden and wished I hadn't accepted and valued the crude comments and jokes I received from the guys in school. Deep down, I thought I wasn't desirable enough to be in a real relationship, and everything else I received from others was all that I was worthy of. But God kept gently reminding me that I should value myself and see myself the way He does, as His chosen daughter, "fearfully and wonderfully made."[1]

Every now and then at church, my dad would say something, or a worship song or scripture verse would stand out to me, and it felt like God was saying, *"Meena, this message is for you. Pay attention."* Over time, I began to realize that the life I was living was not only against the principles of God but was harmful to my emotional wellbeing and to my character. God wanted more for me than the life that I was living.

Even though I felt incredibly alone and unseen during this season, my dad would always notice when something was wrong with me. He'd call me into his office and have these long talks with me to try and help me process whatever I was going through. I never fully alluded to what was going on, but he always knew something was up. Minutes into our conversations, I would be sobbing to him about how I wanted to be better and do better, but

I couldn't figure out how. I didn't know how to stop giving in to the attention and affection from the guys in my life and start living the way God wanted me to. It was like I kept falling into the same cycle of seeking repentance, and then submitting to sin over and over again. It seemed like I just couldn't get it through my head; like I would never figure out how to truly repent and live the life God wanted me to live. After hearing my cries of frustration, my dad would be so patient and loving with me, and each time I would leave his office feeling better.

I'd hear my dad preach about the right way to live, and about how seeking redemption and confessing our sins was very important. Though his messages were filled with truth, I was afraid. I was scared to admit to myself and to God, how far I had fallen away from the little girl who had accepted Christ into her heart almost ten years ago. I didn't know how I could begin to ask for forgiveness and live a life of righteousness. But I knew it was time to try.

While I was struggling to redeem myself and turn my life around, God was already working behind the scenes. I had been touring colleges the entire summer before my senior year and knew that attending a Christian college was going to be the breath of fresh air that I needed. Once I visited Palm Beach Atlantic University, I knew it was the right place for me. The campus, the community, and the professors were a great fit. My faith was stagnant at this point, and I felt like a change in environment and pace of life would help get me on the right track. But before college began, I had the opportunity to leave the country for the first time and experience a depth to my relationship with God that I never had before. I had no idea how much this trip would shape my spiritual life forever.

8 VOLCANOES AND
THE PRESENCE OF GOD

After my first week of senior year, I knew it was time to change things up, once again. My sister Ashley and I weren't too fond of our high school in Mount Vernon and asked our parents if we could be homeschooled for our last year of high school, and they agreed. I enjoyed the challenge of teaching myself the remaining subjects I needed to graduate; and through my own pace of learning, I was able to finish my senior year early, graduating months before summer would begin.

As I was completing my studies in February of 2012, my parents told me about an opportunity to attend the Spanish Language Institute in Costa Rica for the summer. I would be able to learn Spanish and receive college credit, stay with a host family, and build relationships with the missionaries who attended the school. I was excited about the idea, but also very nervous to leave my family for the first time. Everything about this trip was out of my comfort zone, but I knew I needed to get away from home, even if just for a little bit.

My summer in Costa Rica was an experience like no other. Once I arrived in Costa Rica, the drive from the airport left me speechless as I experienced the sights and sounds of the beautiful country. It was like I was seeing the world through fresh eyes. Colors seemed brighter, the air felt cleaner, and the food was fresher and more enjoyable than I imagined! And the land... mountains were everywhere! All the mountains in Costa Rica are so incredibly tall, beautiful, and so majestic. I couldn't help but think, *"no one could have created that except God."* I was mesmerized and captivated by everything that surrounded the mountains and enveloped them. Everything I saw was so new to me, including the building styles, the size of the streets, the road signs with Spanish words on them, the billboards that advertised Costa Rican products, the people, and the music. It was like I had never seen objects, structures, and culture like this in my entire life!

At the Spanish Language Institute, I went to class every day, learning Spanish and participating in the activities and seminars that were given for the missionaries at the school. I was the only one there who wasn't a missionary, yet I was welcomed with open arms by everyone. I was the youngest student there, only eighteen years old at the time, so all of my classmates were at least four to five years older than me. Since we spent so much of our time together, we all quickly became close friends. We went to church together, hung out at restaurants and bars most nights, and on the weekends, we would explore the city of San Jose, sightseeing and shopping. Our group even took numerous trips to visit volcanoes, natural rainforests, and beaches.

I will never forget the trip our group took to visit the Poas Volcano, located in central Costa Rica. We were on an hour-long bus ride to a town that held some of the largest volcanoes in the country. As we were winding up and down the mountains, I looked out the window —- completely captivated. My mind became quiet, and my breath caught in my throat. My gaze was locked on the expanse of the mountains —- the vastness of creation before me. The landscape I saw before me, was of the clouds and the never-ending trail of trees, rocks, and land. All that I could think about was how amazing God was. In that moment, everything around me seemed to melt away. The voices in the bus faded, and all I could feel was the presence of God. I looked out and knew that He was there with me, speaking to me and experiencing this moment with me. I had never felt anything like it before.

Before this, I had only experienced God by trying to understand His Word, the Bible, and the few moments when I would pray to Him about something. But this was different. This was unlike anything I had ever experienced. God was here. He was in creation and all around me. He had created and spoken into existence everything that I was looking at and feeling. He had spoken to me into existence, and in this moment, I understood Him on a deeper level. I knew in my heart that His presence hadn't just "appeared" to me then for the first time but had always been with me. As I looked out the bus window, I knew I was experiencing His creation as the most beautiful and majestic reminder of who He is and the eternality of His presence.

In that moment, my faith felt different, like it was my own for the first time. My relationship with God wasn't just what my parents, my church, or even the world told me it should be. Now, it was up to me, because my faith was my own to believe in and live out. I had my own experience with God, and that was special to me. It felt intimate and precious, and I didn't want to ignore or forget the significance of that moment. I still cherish it close to my heart. God no longer only resided in my mind, but in my heart as well. He became personal to me. He wasn't just someone who I learned about on a Sunday, who I confessed my sins to, who convicted me with truth, and who was Lord over my life. All of that was still true. But now, God was also part of me, within me, and all around me. He was my Friend and my Father. He was someone very close to me. And that fact changed my life forever.

Once again, the colors outside were different. The mountains, volcanos, springs, and the beach were different. Even the people in my life were different and more special to me because I knew they experienced God the same way I did. Now, when my friends and I talked about life and about God together, I connected with them on a deeper level. My perspective and my heart had changed. I had changed.

As my time in Costa Rica came to a close, I had a lot to reflect on and take home with me. My faith had changed forever and my appreciation for life had grown. I wanted to keep discovering how I felt on that bus on the mountain. I wanted to feel exhilarated by looking at creation. I wanted to feel close to God all the time. I wanted to see Him in the little things and have my perspective on life be a bit brighter. I wanted the presence of God to follow me everywhere I went.

After I came back home from my trip in Costa Rica, I felt ready to embark on my next adventure, to start my new life at college. I knew it would be a little scary, and I had no idea what was in store. But I felt more prepared than ever to head out and to have God rock my world again. He had surprised me with Costa Rica, and I was expectant for life to get even better in West Palm Beach, Florida.

9 STRENGTHENING MY FAITH

Costa Rica opened my heart to the presence and peace of God, so college was a fresh start for my faith, a place where I could rediscover the kind of healing that lasts, that restores your soul and revives your faith. So, what better place to begin than Palm Beach Atlantic University, a private, faith-based college in South Florida? Moving away from my family, friends, and home was new, exciting, and scary. I was finally an adult and on my own. But I still needed to learn how to heal from the darkness I had lived in throughout high school. My faith hadn't become a solid foundation in my life yet, so I knew that I needed to rediscover it for myself. But first, I needed to find community.

My college experience was fairly normal: stressful, stressful, and you guessed it, stressful. I was academics-focused, and hesitant to have any kind of a social life. As I started to open up to the new friends I had made in college, I began to realize that there was no judgment, no accusations, and no one who wanted to stop being my friend because of what I'd gone through. Instead, there was compassion, and honest accountability to make sure I invested in my spiritual health. Many nights my friends sat and prayed with me, encouraging me to let my parents into the pain and shame I had endured in high school. I welcomed their friendship, but vulnerability didn't come easily to me. I only shared some of what I had gone through with them — the difficulty of grieving my mother and about the guy I had fallen for. There were other hurtful experiences from my adolescence that I had repressed and couldn't even begin to process with anyone.

I didn't completely block out that I had been severely depressed. I just didn't bring it up to my friends. I think on some level, I didn't understand it myself. I didn't know how to explain what that experience was like in high school. It was hard to say out loud that my frustration, despair, and grief had taken me down a path towards contemplating suicide. Even though I came out of it having survived, I still wasn't sure what my emotions were in the aftermath. How could I explain to my friends that sometimes I still just really hated myself? How could I tell them that sometimes I'd get so angry when I was driving, that I'd hit the steering wheel and scream in the car just to get out the frustration of the day? I didn't know how to give words to the pain I still felt when I would reflect and grieve the last few years.

When I was encouraged by my friends to talk to a counselor-in-training (a student herself), it only reaffirmed the agony I felt when someone asked me about my pain. I didn't want to relive my grief with a stranger, especially when she would only affirm my positive perspectives, instead of just listening to me. I didn't need someone to give me a pat on the back and tell me how awesome it was that I was so happy and well-adjusted after having gone through what I had. I didn't know what I needed, but it wasn't that. I sure as heck didn't feel happy about what I'd gone through. So, for a while, I threw counseling out the window and didn't look back.

After that, I pushed my depression further away from my mind, and refused to think about those dark times. I didn't want to remember that time of my life at all. I was too scared to admit that I had wanted to kill myself — that I had felt so hopeless. I was too embarrassed and ashamed to have felt weak in my own faith. So, I buried it, blocked it out, and never brought it up again. The shame kept me silent for a long time. Until I wrote it out for this book; and I'm so thankful that I did.

I've lived in shame from my past struggles with grief, depression, and suicide, right up until writing about it. Even as I write this chapter, I am still coming out of that shame cloud. Days go by where thoughts like "you don't matter", "you're being dramatic", "you are alone in your pain", "get over yourself", and many others, still try to slip through. But there is a voice stronger than those speaking over me. The voice of my Savior and Redeemer, Jesus. He tells me over and over again that those thoughts are lies from the enemy; and His voice speaks louder than any other voice around.

I find so much solace and reassurance in God's voice. His Word, the Bible, reminds me of truth often. In my quiet times in prayer, I can read about His truth and experience His power working through me to dispel the lies of the enemy, helping me overcome all my greatest fears. It's one of the best feelings in the world. Everything else just melts away, leaving you feeling that without a shadow of a doubt, you can get through the next few minutes, the next hour, and the next day.

I've had some pretty dark seasons, as you've just read about. There is no denying that I've struggled to see the light, the hope, and the joy. But it doesn't mean that it wasn't there. It doesn't mean that God wasn't right there beside me. Even when times seemed to be full of despair, His voice was still there. The voice that is much kinder and speaks with more love than my conscience ever could. His voice that tells me to do the right thing and why; and each time, I know in my heart that saying yes to God is always the best decision I could make. That's the voice of God, the Holy Spirit speaking.

In the darkest moments of my past, in high school especially, I recall knowing that I should have been reaching out and asking for help. But the fear of the unknown and the insurmountable shame was all consuming; to the point that I didn't want to listen to the voice of God speaking to me. I was too afraid of what comes after being vulnerable with Him. Judgment? Accusation? More abandonment? Those lies all spoke louder than the still, gentle voice of God.

But before I could understand that I needed to be healed, I needed to know who the Healer was. Back then, I didn't understand who God was to me. So how could I grasp the fact that I needed Him like I need air in my lungs? I desperately wanted to know God and be known by Him. Desperately.

While in college, I was able to grow my faith as I attended Christ Fellowship Church with my friends, and as I was led in my studies by professors who taught with an abundance of biblical truth. I was beginning to understand what it meant to truly know and love God. Happiness and joy were seeping into my being; but not because of my circumstances, because of Who I was learning to love more than anything.

I don't think I would've understood the slow work that God was doing in me any sooner than in His perfect timing. I couldn't begin to deal with my past, my pain, or my shame until I learned who God was to me and who I was to Him. He, my Father and I, His child. The uprooting and deep healing would come later.

During my second year in college, God convicted me of some healing that needed to take place in my heart, forgiveness. I had a lot to forgive, and God knew that it was time. I was finally ready to forgive my family and friends for not realizing that I was in pain, forgive my mother for dying, forgive God for taking her too soon, and forgive myself for all the shame I held onto because of my own sins.

It took some serious time and patience, but God knew that I was ready. He had prepared my heart to receive forgiveness in the moments where I poured over his Word and the times when I was encouraged by my friends. Scared and unsure of what that would look like, I took the leap and started the work in my heart. There was no handbook to forgiveness next to me. I had more of an understanding from God that if there was any hatred, malice, or ill will toward anyone in my heart, including myself, then I needed to pray over and over that God would heal my heart completely. I needed to be able to think of someone that I had been hurt by, and not have any pain or hatred in my heart towards them. I needed to be able to wish them well, and to genuinely pray for them if I was to forgive them at all. Anything less would be a lie to them and to myself. Day by day, my heart grew softer. My faith was being strengthened and my resolve to hold out for hope grew as well.

There was still more I had to learn about trusting God in all things. College takes you to a whole new level of dependance on the Lord. As I neared my final year at Palm Beach Atlantic, the pressure to know exactly what I would be doing next with my life loomed over me. The job search grew more discouraging by the minute as my last semester of college drew closer. I really believed God was calling me to work in the community of West Palm Beach, specifically with any nonprofit, but my job applications seemed to be passed over left and right. There weren't any places that were looking to hire me; so, my future seemed bleak and unknown, leaving me feeling incredibly lost.

God hadn't forgotten me though; He had an opportunity waiting. But it wasn't anything like what I had been looking for. Instead, it would be everything that I needed; and my life would never be the same again.

PART III

10 ADVENTURE OF A LIFETIME

During my last year of college, I felt less and less sure of what God had in store for me next. So, one day I called my dad for advice. He often gave me a lot of peace and clarity when I struggled to figure out what I was doing with my life, which seemed to be all the time. During our chat, he casually offered up an idea. *What about going to Spain for a year to work with a missionary?* It honestly seemed too good to be true, but I thought I'd at least hear him out.

You see, a few years back my aunt took a trip to Southern Spain to work with a missionary from the Christian Missionary Alliance (the organization that partnered with and supported my dad's church plant). This missionary worked to provide homes, resources, and education for women rescued from human trafficking. My aunt had the most amazing experience serving there, so my dad knew this could be a great experience for me as well. He suggested that I apply for an internship with the Christian Missionary Alliance as a short-term missionary and live in Spain for a year working alongside the same missionary.

Honestly, my first reaction to this possible next step for my future was not excitement, but disinterest. I didn't think this opportunity matched up with the direction I wanted to head in after graduation. Fighting human trafficking was not something I was passionate about at the time, and quite frankly, it scared me. I barely knew anything about human trafficking and thought I wasn't equipped to be on the frontlines (or even behind the scenes) in that ministry environment. I told my dad I'd think and pray about it, but I was sure that wasn't where God was going to send me. All that kept going through my mind was, *"There's no way I could do that. I couldn't leave the country for a whole year. I'm supposed to stay here in South Florida forever. That isn't where God is calling me."*

As the weeks flew by, I realized that my dream of staying in West Palm Beach and living out the rest of my life there was just that, a dream. I knew all of my prayers were heard, but God wasn't opening any doors. In fact, he was closing a lot of them — nearly every single one I tried to walk through. So, I decided to apply for the internship with the Christian Missionary Alliance. Even as I filled out the online application, I fully expected God to shut that door as well. I had grown up in a rigorous school environment, believing that qualifications and experience were the only way that someone would consider you for any kind of opportunity. I didn't think I had anything in my resume that would've shown that I was a good fit for an internship in Spain.

But my perspective on whether I was qualified or not was misguided, God provides the qualifications you need, and He will equip you where He calls you. To my surprise, my application was immediately accepted, and God did provide. The door to Spain was now open, but I continued to have doubts, fueled by my own insecurities and fears. In my prayers, I felt like God wasn't hearing any of them. I tried so hard to tell Him that He was wrong, that this trip wasn't going to work out at all. But He kept providing opportunities for me to continue preparing for Spain. My church in West Palm Beach had recently started a ministry to help spread awareness about human trafficking. So, I jumped at the opportunity to learn from the trainings they offered. The more I learned, the more my heart for grew for Spain and for the work that I could be a part of.

Even after I graduated that May, in 2015, I still wasn't convinced that my trip to Spain was even happening. Fundraising for the internship wasn't progressing well, so I was convinced that it meant God had closed the door indefinitely. I wasn't sure what was going to happen with this possible opportunity, but I could tell that God was doing some important work in my heart. He was teaching me to trust Him for my future in ways I was only just beginning to comprehend.

Once I returned to New York to live with my family after graduation, I had decided to move forward with my trip. I chose to step out in faith that God would continue to provide the resources I needed for to fund my trip.

Since it would take about three months to get my work visa approved and I wasn't planning to leave for Spain until the following January, I decided to sign up for a college course on spiritual disciplines through Nyack College to pass the time. I knew that my time in Spain would transform my personal faith even more, so I decided to be proactive and work on strengthening the foundation of how I spent my time with God. During a two-day retreat our class attended, I began to understand the presence of the Holy Spirit, especially when it came to my grief.

There are many spiritual disciplines we can use to draw closer to God — and I found that a few of them drew me closer to my mother as well. I wasn't expecting this at all, but the closer I felt to the presence of God, the closer I felt to Heaven, and to my mother. It was painful at first, but I knew God was there with me. I desired to be closer to Him, so I knew that even if the process would be hard, it would be worth it.

As our class delved into practicing the discipline of worship (through song and reflection) on our first day of the retreat, I learned to appreciate and welcome the presence of God in a new way. As I worshiped, I felt safe and at home with the Holy Spirit as life's distractions faded around me. For the first time, the presence of God in worship was a calming presence to be in, one that brought beauty and peace to a space that usually held more sorrow and longing. In the past, any time I felt close to experiencing Heaven on earth during worship, I longed for my mother. But this time, worship didn't leave me feeling terribly sad. The closer I drew to God's presence, the more I realized that my mother is always with me when I worship — and I even felt closer to my mother when I worshiped and when I spent time with God. I knew that I didn't need to be afraid to be in His presence and be reminded of my mother at the same time. It was a special and sweet glimpse of Heaven on earth that I could always cling to.

During the second day of the retreat, we practiced the discipline of silence and solitude, which involves listening and quieting your own mind so that you can hear God speaking to you. In the beginning, it took some time for my thoughts to quiet down, and once they had I felt awkward just sitting in complete silence. But as I became more comfortable with the silence, I felt God whisper intimate words of truth to me, words in the form of Psalms I had read or affirmations that I had often struggled to believe about myself. Sitting in silence with God felt less awkward the more I practiced quieting my mind to hear Him. I found myself feeling instantly relaxed and comforted in those moments; not because it was me talking to myself, but because it was my Father in Heaven affirming and freeing me.

In my practices of silence and solitude at the retreat, I couldn't help but reflect on my mother and the grief I felt but couldn't bring myself to deal with yet. I realized that even though I might never understand why He took my mother home to Heaven, I knew that I would never stop praising and worshiping Him — even if He took everything away from me. In those two days away, God became infinitely more important to me than anything and everything in my life because of how my trust in Him and love for Him grew.

When we allow ourselves to sit and embrace the disciplines of the faith, we are willing to let God into our hearts and make our requests known to Him. As we turn to Him, giving Him our everything (our love, our hopes, our longings), He will fill us up with His words of wisdom and love. At one point during the retreat, sitting outside in nature, gazing at the wondrous creation of our Lord, I was left speechless because of what He has to offer us every day as a reminder of who He is. He was continuously showing me so much about Himself through the disciplines I was learning.

I had genuinely missed out on spending time with God in this way, and before the retreat I had no idea why. In my time of reflection after the retreat, I came to learn that I used to hold back from deepening my intimacy with God, because it hurt too much to also be drawn to my mother. Now, the openness to God's heart felt so beautiful and freeing, even though grief was present too. I soon came to realize that this was just the beginning of my renewed relationship with Him. I would need continued strength from God, and confidence in Him, that He would continue to help me through my struggles to be intimate and close to Him. Grief is truly a pain like no other, but I knew that I had God on my side, and His love for me would bring me the courage I needed to move forward.

After the retreat was over, the ninth anniversary of my mother's passing was right around the corner, and the grief still felt incredibly painful. It seemed unending, even pictures and her audiocassettes were more painful than helpful. I didn't want to think about the past and wish she was there with me. At that point, memories tended to bring brief comfort, and then lasting pain. I didn't want to feel that pain, but it seemed like that was just what grieving was for me. I knew God would just have to be with me through it. Once I opened up to Him about my feelings about grief and didn't hold back on how I felt towards Him, His presence never left me. Practicing silence and solitude helped me be able to hear God speak to me clearer than ever before. I knew He was always at work to strengthen our relationship and to mend my heart back to Him. He had never left me, no matter how painful the days had been and might be in the future. I knew the grief might never go away, but I also knew God was going to be with me through it all.

In the blink of an eye, the holidays had arrived and my trip to Spain was only a month away. One night the same missionary my aunt had worked with, my new friend Beth, called with an update and to check in. To my surprise, she shared with me that the family who was supposed to stay with us at her house and help with the ministry, couldn't come any longer. This sudden change of plans greatly affected how our year together was originally supposed to go, because without the additional help, Beth wouldn't be able to expand her ministry as she had hoped to. Therefore, the "behind the scenes" work I would be doing was going to be quite minimal, and I'd have to find other ways to occupy my time in ministry. So, Beth encouraged me to pray about whether I should still head to Spain, since we really had no set plans anymore.

It didn't take long for me to be sure that God still wanted me to say yes to going to Spain. The Holy Spirit worked in my heart quickly to know that I was supposed to go on this trip. Even though the uncertainty was greater, I had confidence that God was still going to use me there. He had been preparing me for this trip, and He knew that I was ready.

11 SPAIN

The rest of Part III recounts one of my favorite stories of transformation and redemption from my life. When I entered Spain, I was still healing from dark seasons of grief where I had lost all sense of who I was. My identity and my security were shattered, and I was only just beginning to pick up the pieces and glue them back together. I was still learning how to truly love myself the way God loves me. I didn't have any idea what He had in store for me; or how He would strip me of everything that I clung to and believed in, so that I could see myself the way He saw me. He had revived in my heart the foundations of my faith while I was in college. Now the painful work would begin in understanding myself as a child of God, and learning how to live that out in a world where suffering is ongoing. When I tell people that I came back from Spain a completely different person, you'll see why. God truly transformed my life from the inside out.

Cracking the shell

As I set out on my trip to Spain, I'll admit I had some doubts that God was going to show up for me, but He quickly dissuaded those during my connecting flight to Paris, France. When I woke up in the middle of the flight and glanced out my window to see the sun rise over a foggy Eiffel Tower, I recalled one huge reason I had decided to take this trip in the first place. I chose to embark on this journey to grow closer to God and to experience Him more fully, in a new and exciting way. And here I was, already seeing His creation, His world, as He originally made it. How beautiful it was to see! During the night, I had gone to sleep flying over the ocean, and arose the next morning in a new country where the day was just beginning. That was the moment I truly fell in love with travel. My heart calmed and the impending excitement grew to see Spain, and to experience and know God like never before. He had shown up before I had even reached my first destination, before my layover, and before I even flew into Spain.

As my second flight was descending into Malaga, Spain, I could see the ocean, the beautiful, bright blue with a hint of green ocean, and a vast array of mountains completing the gorgeous landscape. The plane made a wide circle so that I could see the entire city, the mountains filled with whitewashed homes, and the shore of the ocean all at once. It was breathtaking.

After I landed in Malaga and Beth picked me up at the airport, I was able to experience Spain for the first time. I never wanted to stop exploring it all. The air was beautiful, the environment wide and vast, and all of it, God's creation. That was the most surreal experience of all, constantly falling in love with His creation all around me.

A couple days into my trip, I quickly realized that I couldn't just jump into the work I would be doing immediately. I had to adjust to the culture and way of life in Spain, which valued rest and time with family more than work, seemingly opposite of America's culture and way of life. For the first three months in Spain, I spent most of my time exploring Malaga, and learning to improve my Spanish. I also spent a lot of time getting to know Beth. Life with her was full of genuine community and love because she quickly treated me like one of her daughters. She cared about my heart and about my relationship with God more than the work she wanted me to be doing. It was a refreshing friendship. I didn't realize how much I needed her in my life to help me heal and grow. Before long, we began sharing about our lives and our pasts with each other. Within the first week of my trip, I had shared everything about losing my mother and about my experience of grief with Beth.

One evening, Beth started talking to me about going through the process of inner healing with her, which simply put is, taking time to understand and heal from any past hurts or experiences you may have. She knew how important it was for me to learn how to grieve the loss of my mother and process memories from my childhood in a healthy way. So, she encouraged me to think about processing my inner healing through the guidance of Pete Scazzero's teachings from his book, *Emotionally Healthy Spirituality*. Beth offered to help me each step of the way, but I wasn't completely sure I was ready to walk through inner healing yet. The thought of jumping into vulnerability with anyone felt like an impossible feat to overcome, especially when it came to sharing about my mother. I knew I needed to be comfortable sharing stories of my life with Beth first, before I could be ready to trust her with the deeper parts of myself.

Beth respected my reluctancy, treated me with kindness, and was patient with me as I spent weeks in prayer over whether to start working on my healing with her. It didn't take long for me to know that I could trust her. She reminded me a lot of my dad because she knew when to press in when I brought up my insecurities, fears, and worries. She also knew exactly how to check in with me and to ask the deep questions that would cause me to think introspectively. She quickly became one of the people in my life who instantly knew how my mind worked, and how my emotions and my tendencies manifested themselves. Beth was someone very in tune with the Spirit of God. God knew I needed her in my life. Within a couple weeks of knowing Beth, I knew I could trust her because I could experience for myself how she let the Holy Spirit lead her words and actions.

Right before I was ready to start the inner healing process, I became more intentional about sitting in silence and solitude with God. I wanted to be at peace with making the decision to seek healing for my past hurts and losses, those I knew of and those I had yet to discover. I knew this process wouldn't be a piece of cake. I would be purposely putting myself through pain to find lasting healing, but I knew God would be there with me. I just needed to trust Him and believe that He would be there through it all, encouraging me to take the next step.

Many mornings I would go spend time at a small park near the house I was living at, with the most breathtaking view of the mountains and the land of Andalucía (the Southernmost region of Spain where we lived), and just talk to God. I developed a good rhythm of just spending time with God to continue strengthening our relationship. Seeing the beautiful pictures that God paints in nature, whether it be the mountains, the ruins of architectural history, the Mediterranean Sea, or a majestic sunset or sunrise, would remind me of how great and loving our God is. A true glimpse of hope for what is yet to come, and what we can find comfort in through Him when all the world seems bleak. Fully surrendering to the healing process didn't seem as daunting and scary knowing that God was right there beside me, guiding me through every step.

During my time with God, He would often reassure me that I was ready to start opening myself up to healing, emotionally and spiritually. As I spent countless hours with Him, God would remind me that even the worst part of our story is where He can use us to show how great and powerful His love is.

But the idea of this process was still overwhelming. At times I saw it as wrought with shame and self-doubt. I'd feel like this heavy weight had fallen on me as I thought about the fear and shame that might come up if I were to bring up old wounds. It felt like the fact that I had to go through this healing, meant that all the issues I had were my own fault. I felt like there was something wrong with me because of everything that had happened in my life.

In those moments of doubt, God would regularly remind me that there wasn't anything wrong with me. This was hard to believe at first because for as long as I could remember, I believed that I needed to fix myself. I believed that because my future wasn't where I wanted it to be, with a successful career and a family of my own, and because my past had broken me in more ways than one, that meant that something was wrong with me. So, God needed to fix me, or I needed to change something about myself.

But the more I felt frustrated by the idea of processing my past and healing from it, the more drawn I was to spend time with God. I felt like I just couldn't avoid how I was feeling about myself anymore. I knew that God wanted me to heal from my past and see myself the way He always saw me. So, each time I felt overwhelmed, I knew I needed to spend more time with Him and soak in His truth.

Reading and meditating on Romans 9:20-21 helped me remember who I am to God. When God made us, He did not make a mistake. We are who we are because He made us in that way. He has purpose in our existence because He made us. There are no mistakes or mess-ups when it comes to our lives because we are His children and He will use us as He always intended, no matter what. I still had trouble believing that truth, but I hoped that while I was in Spain, I would feel more of God's truth and love within me.

As I sought to understand that I am not a mistake and that it is not up to me to "fix" my circumstances, I came to realize and rest in the fact that I can't do anything or have anything in this life without God. I needed to stop trying to improve myself, and just surrender myself into His arms completely. I needed to start practicing that by talking to Him as soon as I started to feel impatient, irritated, and anxious instead of remaining in a constant state of distress. I knew that my foundation had to be centered on God; He needed to be the first person I went to whenever I was dealing with some aspect of my past and trauma. If I didn't trust Him to care and comfort and protect me in this process, then I would give up on my own healing completely. And I didn't want to give up. I was ready to begin the inner healing process no matter how hard it would be.

The following chapters will take you through the inner healing journey I experienced as I studied one of Scazzero's seminars from *Emotionally Healthy Spirituality*. Scazzero's book takes the reader through a guided process of understanding biblical principles, and their story, to find lasting emotional and spiritual healing. I highly recommend you add his book to your bookshelf, not only because it shaped most of my healing journey, but because it also helped me understand that only the absolute truth and unconditional love of Christ could bring me the healing I was searching for. So, let's jump in.

12 FOUNDATIONS OF INTIMACY WITH GOD

What is Your Story?

Over the years, I've had numerous opportunities to share with others the story of how I grew up, what happened when my mother got sick and died, how that affected me, and everything in between. As I began learning how important healing is, and why I needed to face my story, accept, and thereby love it, I knew that I needed to practice sharing my story more. After getting closer to Beth and sharing more about my mother and my grief with her, I came to find that it was becoming a little easier to share my story with her. The grief and sorrow I felt each time I talked about my mother wasn't as painful, and my heart didn't hurt as much. I was beginning to see my story the way that God sees it, as beautiful and as redemptive as it was meant to be.

But it took some time for me to see God's perspective on my story. The year I spent in Spain, processing and redeeming the dark and hard spaces in my life, stripped me of every lie I had believed about myself and about my story since I was a kid, which was no small feat. But starting at the beginning to redefine my identity in Christ helped me to differentiate between the lies of the enemy, that told me my story was full of brokenness and would always be, and the truth of God, who says my story was full of beauty and redemption.

I encourage you to embrace your community and tell your story often. When I say, "your story", I mean the events that shaped and wounded you, the lies you might have believed about yourself and about God, and the family patterns and hurts you've experienced thus far. It's scary to reveal deep, vulnerable parts of yourself with another person, and even more so with a group of people you may not know very well. But your community was given to you by God for a reason. He wants you to be able to trust them with parts of yourself you love *and* the parts you hate. The parts you understand *and* the parts you wish didn't exist. Invite them into your life and share that life with them. Confess and be healed with them.

Processing through your story with others can help you embrace and learn from your relationships, your family, the painful points in your story, the blessings and joys you've experienced, the spiritual encounters (positive and negative) that have shaped you, and the tragedies and losses you have gone through. All these aspects of your life need to be embraced and processed so that you can find emotional and spiritual healing.

If you avoid processing events like these from your story, over time you may find that you've unintentionally invited triggers of your past to disrupt your life. When I avoided my grief and neglected to deal with the past hurts I had experienced in high school, there were many moments I could recall from college where my behavior didn't match how I felt inside. There were many times where I would quickly overreact to seemingly minimal issues. The more I avoided how I was feeling about a conversation or a situation that had triggered my past, the more often my emotions would get the better of me. For example, often while driving to class, I would find myself getting so angry at the car in front of me for driving too slowly that I'd curse at them and beat on the steering wheel (also known as road rage), or while at home I would curse and shame myself for simply forgetting to take the garbage can out before work. These are all overreactions that were not necessarily related to why I was even upset. They were triggers of underlying issues that I hadn't processed yet. Back in college, I didn't understand why I acted and reacted the way I did. But I began to understand that it was because I chose to avoid dealing with my own pain. Until I was honest with myself, I wouldn't be ready to do the work to find deeper intimacy with God and work my way towards achieving emotionally healthy spirituality.

Speaking from my own experience, I believe it'll get easier the more you share your story with others. You'll start to see yourself healing before you realize it's happening. Then, your story won't bring you immeasurable pain as you tell it, but joy that only comes from the Lord.

Do you Know Your Own Soul?

Once I understood the importance of sharing my story, I began to see how broken my perspective on life truly was. Before I could even begin to process my past, I needed to first learn how to be self-aware. As we grow in self-awareness, we are able to truly know our own soul and the inner workings of our emotions and actions. As followers of Jesus, that growth starts with walking in the light, in His light.

> 1 John 1:5-7 says, "This is the message we have heard from him and proclaim to you, that God is light, and in him is not darkness at all. If we say we have fellowship with him while we walk in darkness, we lie and do not practice the truth. But if we walk in the light, as he is in the light, we have fellowship with one another, and the blood of Jesus his Son cleanses us from all sin."

We need to be willing to walk in the light, confess, and remain with and in God. But how do we do this? We admit everything about ourselves to Him. Present the real you, not the "you" who you wish you were, so that you can receive and accept His true love. Until we are completely honest with God about everything (our thoughts, our desires, our sins, etc.), we won't be able to heal our souls and receive true intimacy with Him. You can't build a truly committed and healthy relationship with someone if you aren't completely honest with that person, right? The same goes for your relationship with God. Don't hold back, He knows everything about you because He created you. He knew our past, present, and future before we even took our first breath. He wants to grow a deep and lasting relationship with you, so invite Him in.

We also need to press into what our identity is to be self-aware and to know our soul deeply. Our identity is something that we receive from God, not something that is given to us or forced upon us by society. Our identity is solely in Him because He created us in His image. So, to know ourselves, we need to know God fully. Start by desiring to know Him deeper through worship, by reading His Word, by being in community, and by practicing the spiritual disciplines. Be intentional about spending time with God to encounter His presence and truth, and to get to know Him personally. The more time you spend with Him, the more He'll teach you about Himself, and the more you'll learn about yourself as His child.

Growing Your Intimacy with God

In the beginning I viewed the entire inner healing process as a task I needed to achieve and be good at, so I assumed that growing and deepening my relationship with Him meant doing more for Him or being better. Growing my intimacy with God seemed daunting, leaving me feeling like I would fail before I even started. It was so easy to doubt that I could learn how to "be better" at my relationship with God.

I gave myself the excuses that it was because I didn't have the biblical knowledge or life experience to be better, I didn't have the time, or I wouldn't be good at it. But this wasn't a class I needed to pass or a job I needed to have qualifications to apply for. In this case, the only thing I needed was God to achieve intimacy with Him! Through prayer, I sought God's reassurance that He was going to be with me and that ultimately, He would help me grow my intimacy with Him. I couldn't focus on my own inadequacies because He would provide everything that I needed to start this healing process. At the end of the day, I didn't need the qualifications, the extra time in my day, or the skills to achieve intimacy with God. I just needed to decide to do it and then, just do it. Just decide to spend time with God in any way that works for you (like the spiritual disciplines I mentioned a couple chapters back), and you've already done what He's called you to do.

We need Him. With Him, we can achieve the impossible. He makes all things possible. We need to keep pursuing God, especially when we felt inadequate. We need His strength and the power of the Holy Spirit to change us from the inside out. Our hearts need to become like His, so that we can see ourselves the way that He sees us. True intimacy with the Father starts by seeing Him as someone we can be close and intimate with. He needs to be our closest personal friend. He needs to be our everything.

Your Daily Rhythms

As we seek to know God deeper, our intimacy with Him will grow when we spend more time with Him in various daily rhythms, specifically the spiritual disciplines of the faith. Pursuing God through practicing the spiritual disciplines can help our thoughts and actions be emotionally and mentally led by God instead of by our sinful human nature. As we spend more time with God, our thoughts and our actions will be more like His character, further deepening our intimacy with Him.

Practicing silence and solitude (being alone with God) regularly is one of my favorite ways to grow in intimacy with God. Solitude stills the soul and prepares the heart by bringing self-awareness and God-awareness. This takes some practice if you aren't used to spending intentional time by yourself. When I was first learning how to practice silence and solitude, I had to learn how to quiet my heart and my mind completely to really prepare myself to just be with God. Our minds run a mile a minute, so being silent without thinking about anything at all is hard at first. Especially for someone like me who is always in her head. I tend to think and overthink everything all the time! But after practicing silence and solitude for a couple weeks, I found that instead of it taking 20 minutes to quiet my soul so that I could begin to be with God in complete silence on my own, it only took a couple of minutes to quiet my soul.

When you spend consistent time in silence for an extended period of time, you can hear the still voice of God, through the work of the Holy Spirit. For some people it is auditory, for others it feels like the presence of God is with you and you don't hear anything. For me, as I practiced silence more regularly, I could hear the voice of God as well. Now I'm not an expert in practicing this discipline, but I knew I was hearing the voice of God because words, phrases, and affirmations that spoke to the character of God were audible in my head. They reached and calmed my heart. Words that were meant for me, and words that are also found in scripture, were in my mind without my own prompting. His truths became a further confirmation of His presence around me and in me. I knew He was with me, but I also felt like my soul was being heard by God. He knew the innermost desires, worries, and prayers of my heart before I even voiced them, before I even knew what I wanted to say to Him. This experience grows a longing for God that cultivates a desire to hear and surrender to Him continually. Honestly, it's one of the most beautiful experiences I have ever had with God. I strive to have that intimacy and depth with Him all the time.

Another rewarding aspect of practicing silence and solitude is that the more you do it, the more you want to do it. The more time you want to spend with God, the closer in intimacy you grow to be with Him. As you continue to abide in Him, you bear the fruit of deepening in intimacy with Him — knowing that you are loved and cherished by God, fulfilling His purpose for your life.

It's important to find a regular routine of practicing the spiritual disciplines. You don't have to do all of the spiritual disciplines every day, but find the disciplines that connect you with God best. For me, it was silence and solitude, reading His word, and worshiping with Him in nature and in community. You can also fast, meditate on His word, pray, study the Word, and spend time in service, confession, hospitality, and celebration. There are several different spiritual disciplines, and they are all beneficial to deepening your intimacy with God. You may find that some are more helpful in certain seasons of your life, while others aren't as helpful. Find what works for you and regularly practice spending time with God.

If you find yourself reluctantly spending time with God because it's become monotonous or too repetitive (and this does happen), break rhythms that are detrimental and start rhythms that bring you closer to Him. Mix it up and try new things. Pick up a new spiritual discipline and see how that one feels. Bring other people and your community into practicing your spiritual disciplines with you.

Suffering and Sacrificing to Grow

We grow in deeper intimacy with God even while we suffer, because our relationship with Him is greatly shaped by how we suffer. We can either choose to let God into our suffering, try to get through it all on our own, or avoid it completely. All suffering is part of life, and we will experience suffering, not just once, but ongoing suffering for the rest of our lives. There is sin in this world and until Jesus returns to bring the new heavens and new earth, we will continue to experience sorrow and pain.[2]

But how does suffering grow our intimacy with God and bless us? Suffering develops substance and depth of soul within us as we lament and grieve our pain. It takes time to accept suffering and receive true redemption from it. God will always provide redemption for our suffering; we just need to be patient and let Him bring us through it in His timing. When we lament, we are inviting God into our suffering. Instead of asking God why you are suffering, ask Him how He will redeem it. Question how God is teaching you and let Him respond with His love for you.

You may not see it yet, but God has redemption and joy for your suffering. He won't let you suffer without bringing a way to bless you through it. Our relationship with God is a partnership, so let Him be there for you. Invite Him in and let Him bring peace to situations that have no peace, light to the darkest places, and joy to the most heartbreaking of circumstances.

Lastly, we can grow in intimacy with God through our sacrifices. We need to practice sacrificing for God with a heart of love. Sacrifice your worldly desires, and your heart, to reach the dream He has for you. For me, that meant coming to terms with the reality that I needed to submit and release the people in my life to God completely. I am continually reminded of the story in Genesis 22 where Abraham had to sacrifice his son Isaac, knowing that God would still be faithful in His promise through the covenant He established in Genesis 17.³ The people we have in our lives are not ours, the Lord can give, and the Lord can take away. But He always keeps His promises.

Once I understood the sacrifice of giving the people in my life to God fully, I was still left thinking, *"what's the point of pursuing and experiencing love from others if there's a possibility of losing them?"* Sometimes it feels too hard to risk loss for love, especially as someone who lost loved one who meant the world to me. I knew the reality of what it felt like to lose someone I loved, so it felt too scary to love anyone the same again. It seemed like everyone I had ever loved had left me one way or another. But part of learning and discovering more about God and growing in intimacy with Him, was about finding the answer and the peace to that question.

So, what's the point of pursuing and experiencing love from others when you could possibly lose that love? I would tell myself now that those relationships are worth the risk. Sacrificing without knowing what the future holds isn't meant to be easy, it's meant to challenge you and draw you closer to God as you seek to understand what exactly He's calling you into.

In the beginning of this healing process, I still struggled to believe the truths that God was teaching me. I had fears, worries, and doubts that God would even come through for me. At the deepest core of myself, I believed that I was meant to be alone forever because I hated the idea of risking loss for love, even though I knew the truth of God like the back of my hand. We know, hear, and somewhat understand what God is teaching us, but in our hearts and minds, sometimes the story is not the same. I still needed to learn to rewrite God's truth over my own.

Matthew 16:25 says, "For whoever would save his life will lose it, but whoever loses His life for my sake will find it." You must sacrifice everything from your old life for the depth of intimacy that God freely gives, because that's what being a follower of Christ means —— you are agreeing to no longer follow the ways of this world anymore. You're not "halfway in", you're all in. Be all in with God. Trust that He is someone worth sacrificing all our fears of loneliness and abandonment to, knowing that with Him we are never truly alone. He provides love and security in more ways than we can fathom. Wholeheartedly trust in God to receive His intimacy. Give your everything to receive everything that God has to offer.

13 GROWING TRUST AND FAITH

During the summer, I had the opportunity to serve several different ministries in a few cities in Spain and Portugal, growing my trust in God as He led me to step out of my comfort zone. Within a couple of months, I had volunteered at two summer camps, visited a church plant, and served with a ministry that supported single Muslim mothers. I was able to receive glimpses of the character of God in others and in the person He created me to be. He answered many of my small prayers, that I would be stretched and challenged that summer. He gave me a joy for the culture of Spain, which is "work to live", to just enjoy where I am at in life, and to approach life as a child — with no worries or concerns about the things I couldn't control. With this different mindset, I felt free to spend countless hours with God as I explored new towns, cleared my head, and just slowed down. God always showed me something new to discover about Himself, myself, or my mother on those walks. I loved the slowed down life in Spain, and really embraced experiencing God in His creation.

Trusting God and His Character

As I continued learning from Scazzero's teachings, I spent many mornings reading the book of Genesis to find verses that spoke of God's love, but instead I came to find verses that spoke of the trust He instills in those He makes His promises to. In Genesis 17:15-19, God tells Abraham that Sarah will bear a child in her old age to fulfill His covenant promise that Abraham would be a father of many nations. While it seemed unlikely because of her age, this passage reminds us that we should trust in God's promises because He is the one who will fulfill them, not us. He is the reward we seek, and we cannot let anything (even our own doubts) stand in the way of receiving Him and His promises for us.

As time progressed, and as I began to trust God more, He revealed to me some areas within my heart that still needed to be redeemed. He showed me that I still held a lot of anger towards Him, and I knew why. For a long time, I felt like God had taken my childhood away from me when my mother was sick. I had to grow up a lot sooner than I should have as I cared for my mother on my own and helped make my own life decisions that should never have been my role to make (choosing my own guardians). I often blamed God for that season of my life even though it wasn't His fault that she was sick and died, it wasn't anyone's fault. It didn't feel right to be mad at God, even though that's how I felt. I knew that I needed to address how I felt towards Him if I ever wanted to move forward in my life to receiving healing. In his book, Scazzero says, "how can we listen to what God is saying and evaluate what is going on inside when we cut ourselves off from our emotions?"[4] I had always believed that being angry and sad were sinful emotions, and that God didn't want me to express them. But I needed to embrace my feelings and know that God embraced them as well.

We have to understand that "our feelings are a component of what it means to be made in the image of God."[5] If we don't go to Him with our anger, we'll never understand the root of why we are angry, and we won't be able to understand an important aspect of the character of God. He communicates with us through our feelings. Emotional health means "experiencing the full weight of your feelings... don't censor them... God will come to you through them."[6]

Through this discovery, I realized that my anger towards God also came from constantly avoiding my own grief whenever I was around other people who were suffering. Any suffering that resembled sickness reminded me too much of how my mother struggled and how painful that was to witness. I would get trapped in time and just flashback to my mother throwing up or seizing; I hated remembering those experiences and how I felt back then. It had gotten to the point where I even hated hearing about someone desiring for a miracle to happen to cure someone's illness. All that did was remind me that my mother didn't receive her miracle (beating the cancer), even though many people were praying for her. I'd get so mad and shut down when anyone talked about praying for miracles. I knew it could be God's will for that miracle to not happen. So, it was hard to empathize with others in those moments because all I could think about was that I didn't get what I prayed for. I had trusted that God had a plan for my mother's life, and He gave me peace about her death when she passed, but that didn't mean

I didn't miss her immensely and wish she had lived.

In my times of my reflecting, I'd think about my mother and how losing her impacted how I looked at life. One night during my prayers with God, He reminded me that everyone gets sick, and everyone dies. We are here to do what we can to care for them before God calls them home. We don't have to do that on our own, we have God with us. We can be there for the people in our life, and trust in His plan for them. Talking with God about my anger and hurt instead of holding it in allowed me to listen to His voice and hear His perspective and love for me. As I learned to embrace my emotions and give them to God, I found myself more willing to trust Him and further deepen our relationship.

Trust God for what He is doing, has done, and will do. See the future from His perspective. God is in charge. He sees what we don't, He knows what we may or may not need to know. Reside in the simplicity of trusting in Him for everything. Be patient with yourself; redefining truth takes time.

How Your Faith Shapes You

When my faith began as a young child, I didn't view Christianity as legalistic or full of judgments. I just viewed it as a breath of fresh air because it gave me hope. As I matured in my faith, Christianity wasn't just a religion to me anymore, but a relationship between myself and God. When I struggled with sin and conviction in high school, I started to feel far from God for the first time. It grew more difficult to let God into my fears and into my frustrations as I changed before my own eyes, which made it hard to trust that He would still love me whenever I would sin. I'd end up in this rabbit hole of failure and self-doubt. The cycle would be endless because all my hope for redemption was placed on myself, and not on God. But I couldn't see it that way yet.

Over time surrendering to God and releasing control over my life to Him grew harder to do. I kept basing His acceptance of me on my results and my behaviors; but I could never measure up to my own impossibly high standards that I believed were also God's standards for me. As I looked back on my past, I realized that my security should have been based on His love for me, not on my performance.

Everything about my faith seemed to be founded on what I brought to the table, which would have never been enough anyway. So, of course I was constantly failing and feeling like I could never measure up. I wasn't meant to.

My existence needed to revolve around believing that there wasn't anything I needed to do to receive God's blessings, and that there wasn't anything I did to receive the failures in my life either. I participate in His work, not the other way around.

Our efforts need to be about God, not about us or about other's opinions of us. He sees and rewards us in Heaven. We perform for God alone. We work for His value alone. Don't let yourself be subject to pride, and the lies the enemy tells you about yourself.

I knew it was vitally important to believe these truths about God — that His love is unconditional and that He keeps His promises to be with us. The hard road of healing and discovering my identity in Christ was not over yet.

14 DOES THE ENEMY HAVE A FOOTHOLD

Identity Lies

Whether we realize it or not, there are a lot of lies we may believe to be true about ourselves, and we could be operating in them regularly. It might be easy to be comfortable with who you are (the good and the bad) and resign yourself to staying the same kind of person forever. But God calls us higher than that. As we seek to understand our identity in Christ, we need to understand that what we act on (whether it's the truth or the lies) establishes our foundation. It is vital that we replace the lies we believe about ourselves with the undeniable truth of who Christ says we are, to be free.

Romans 12 explains that by renewing, or retraining, your mind you can understand and live out God's will for your life.[7] We must let God work in us to replace the lies of this world with His truth, so that our foundation in Christ can be solidified. God doesn't promise that it will be easy, but we are being transformed into a living sacrifice and a new creation for Him as we fight the lies of the enemy.

This renewal process takes time and patience. When we have lived believing lies the enemy tells us about ourselves for so long, we are operating from our false self. Our false self is the part of ourselves that has a faulty foundation because we may believe the lies of the enemy so much that our identity is shaped by them.

A performance-based false self may tell you that the issue of your value is determined by your performance — by how well you do at performing a task or achieving a goal. A religious or moral performance-based false self may tell you that making mistakes is not acceptable, leaving you believing that you need to succeed or perform perfectly to be accepted or valued by others.

A people-pleasing false self may tell you that the issue of your value is dependent upon whether people love you. You might feel like certain people, or all people, need to like or love you. We need to understand that if people don't like us, God will always love us. His love needs to be sufficient; we can't depend solely on the love of others. Humans are fallible, not God. People pleasing may tell us that we will receive acceptance based on how we act, what we do, and what we say. Our acceptance and value should not come from or be dependent on others, it should only come from God. His love is the only faithful and dependable love.

I struggled with these identity lies often as a child, especially before coming to Christ. Each day I would make a list of the things I had done wrong and would vow to be perfect the next day, failing every time. But what I had to understand is that God doesn't call us to be perfect, He is perfect. We don't have to be, nor will we ever be, because we are human, and He is God. And guess what, He loves us no matter what.

It seemed easy to discover which identity lies showed up in my life the most, but I still needed to process how they operated fully. First, it was important for me to determine where my defensiveness came from. I would always get defensive when people said they didn't like me (people pleasing lie), or when I was told I was wrong about something I said or did (performance-based lie). I'd quickly get upset and retreat because my pride was too wounded to bother confronting the situation.

Second, I needed to be honest about what identity lie my pettiness was rooted in, and what bothered or annoyed me about others. I found myself constantly bothered by seeing laziness manifest in others and in myself (which attributes to a performance false self), and I'd be easily irritated if others didn't accept or approve of me (which attributes to a people pleasing false self). It became a pet peeve of mine to be around people who were extremely lazy, or people who didn't seem to care about my thoughts or opinions. Performance mattered a lot to me, like how well I performed or excelled and how well other people did, I needed people to be pleased with me, and I needed for others to be pleased with themselves.

Third, I had to understand what I feared I would be missing out on in my life or what I needed the most of, out of life? I discovered that I missed and needed people, close people, in my life and consistent work. I couldn't function or feel like I was operating at my best self if I didn't have those things in my life regularly. Again, performance and people pleasing identity lies emerge.

Lastly, I asked myself where did my security, validation, or affirmation (or lack of) come from? I thankfully had a good childhood and a loving mother, but at an early age she put high expectations on me, which I later continued to put on myself. I didn't realize it at the time, but I often felt pressured by my mother to succeed well above average in school — to become the perfect daughter and student. I don't think I even realized why I was so insecure and lacking in self-confidence until I went through this healing process. Over time, the performance false-self and people pleasing false-self became my normal identities.

Your past can define you at your core, whether you're aware of it or not. How you grew up shapes you in more ways than one, and it's important to acknowledge that. When we take the time to understand and accept how we grew up, we are taking essential steps to find emotional healing, redemption, and hope. This will pave the way for us to start believing who God has created us to be. Just because I was a perfectionist and never felt like I could live up to my own (and others') expectations, that didn't mean that I was doomed to live my life that way forever. I just need to understand where I came from, and to accept how God was going to redeem that part of my story to use it for His glory.

As I reflected on my past, I realized that many phrases I spoke aloud to myself that were demeaning, had latched onto my identity. I could recall daily telling myself, *"I'm not perfect, I need to work harder to get to that person's level"*, *I'm not lovable, I'll never be accepted"*. I honestly believed those lies, because they all made complete logical sense to me. Words have significant power over your mind. Don't let them.

2 Corinthians 10:5 says, *"We destroy arguments and every lofty opinion raised against the knowledge of God and take every thought captive to obey Christ."* Arguments

and lofty opinions that are against the knowledge of God include the demeaning thoughts that have been said to and about you, and that you tell yourself. They are not true, and they are not of God. It is important to rebuke those and replace those thoughts with words and phrases of truth from scripture. What God says about us is true, not what others say about us or what we may say about ourselves to ourselves.

Pay attention to your self-talk, especially if you find that you voice faulty beliefs (like subconscious phrases that keep tearing you down) to yourself. For example, if I messed up on something or something didn't go according to plan, I'd tell myself, *"You idiot, I can't believe you made that mistake! You should've done (blank)!"* What I needed to start teaching myself to do whenever something like that happened, was to ball up those phrases, throw them away, and ask God to give me new phrases. It's important and vital for your emotional health to hold onto God's teaching and His truth. He has more power to renew your mind than you can operating in your own power.

We can't find rest in believing the lies about ourselves, there is no freedom from that. Lies are faulty core values, and they deeply impact our value and our worth. We may easily act as if those lies are truths about us, even when we read and know God's Word. If the lies are ingrained so deep within our soul and life, we may not realize the hold they have on us. The lies could become more than just our identity, they could become the only thing we know to be true about ourselves. When we live that way every single day, we may not realize that we have faulty core values and beliefs.

When our value is broken down over the course of a long time, we may start to see the effect of shame and inadequacy manifest in our lives. Everything about our existence is tainted with lies from the enemy when we live believing we have little or no value. So, we may walk with our heads down, completely devoid of hope. Without God's truth, we might find these and other reasons for why we are not valued by ourselves and others. We may tell ourselves that it's all our fault that we are this way. Over and over again. *"It's my fault I'm not perfect. It's my fault that this person doesn't like me. It's my fault this happened outside of my control."*

The more I avoided dealing with these identity lies, the more I continued to people-please to maintain control and acceptance in my life. It was always my goal to fix myself instead of seeking help to deal with the shame and inadequacy I felt, but I only ended up hurting others and myself in the process. "Unhealed wounds open us up to habitual sin against God and others."[8] God doesn't call us to live in the lies, He calls us to live in the truth that He provides.

In order to stop believing the lies and keep from living out the wrong identity, we need to believe that the issue of our value was settled at the cross because we are worthy of the Son's sacrifice for our life. We have to position the value of God's love as the foundation of our identity. We cannot place our identity and worth on the opinions and approval of others, only on a perfect God who loves us even though we are not, and can never be, perfect.

Scazzero says in *Emotionally Healthy Spirituality*, "Many of us know the experience of being approved for what we do. Few of us know the experience of being loved for being just who we are."[9] "Knowing God's love and acceptance provides the only sure foundation for loving and accepting our true selves."[10]

First, to seek redemption and truth in your identity, you need to identify the lies that you believe. Name them, understand how they show up, and how they make you feel. Identify when you are feeling emotions like anger, self-loathing, frustration, or disappointment. For example, I noticed that I would get anxious whenever I thought about my need to be perfect, or when I would begin to talk down to myself for any mistake I had made.

Recognize when you are acting on a faulty foundation of lies so that you can hold onto the truth and be released from the lies. For example, if you find yourself needing to control the circumstances around you, the deeper emotion underneath that you are feeling might be a fear of rejection and disappointment. To heal from that identity lie and faulty foundation, you can find a word of truth or a phrase from God (in scripture) that you can understand and believe to be true. It should be something that takes you to a place of truth when you feel the trigger of the lies.

Search scripture and provide yourself with an easy-to-remember verse or phrase that points you back to the truth of the gospel, and to God's unchanging love for you. Allow the Holy Spirit to administer His love to you through that verse or phrase. Act in courage of the truth foundation that surrounds and redefines the lie for you.

The repeated action that comes from living out that truth and belief will move the knowledge of God's truth to conviction of His word in your heart. Don't avoid combatting the lies with the truth of God. If telling yourself that you are loved and worthy causes you feel the opposite, press into that. Ask yourself why you feel that way when you think of love towards yourself. Don't leave it unresolved even though it hurts to open that particular wound. Press in, it's worth it. Then, you will be able to renew your mind fully and therefore change the way you think about yourself. Hold onto His teaching throughout the process. You can't retrain your mind and heart without remaining steadfast in your dependance on the Lord. Only He can redeem and heal.

Toxic shame

If you find yourself struggling to redefine identity lies, then you may also have some deeper identity wounds that have been invading and poisoning your identity for a long time. It may feel like there is a hole that you keep trying to get filled, but it's going nowhere. Maybe you struggle to accept affirmations and love, and it feels like they just go in one ear and out the other.

There may be multiple reasons for this, maybe there was emotional neglect or trauma in your childhood or during your developmental years. As a result, you might feel the stain of toxic shame on your soul. Toxic shame takes shame to another level and detrimentally affects how you see yourself; it completely shapes your identity and self-worth. For example, I used to think negatively about myself often. I would regularly tell myself that there was something wrong with me. To be honest, I still find myself believing that particular lie, especially during times of significant change or loss.

If some of those lies resonate with you, take a second to ask yourself: *What are the lies you believe? How do they manifest in your life?* Until you stop and answer those questions, it may be hard to move forward into true healing and redemption.

Scazzero explains how symptoms of toxic shame can look like negative self-talk, self-destructive behavior (i.e., self-harm, over-eating), internal judgment, or spiraling self-analysis. Toxic shame can even affect your relationship with God. I remember early in my college years, I felt like I understood God's love for me, but I just couldn't experience it, or it didn't seem to last in my heart. Something wasn't letting me truly feel loved by God. Sometimes I would even try to confess the same sin, but I would have trouble accepting that my sin was forgiven. I couldn't seem to accept God's love and forgiveness towards me.

The roots of toxic shame can include belittlement in your home in the past, emotional or physical abuse, a perception of abandonment or loss), exposure to a culture of performance and the pressure to perform to receive love and acceptance, or continual sinful behavior (with an accumulation of sin and shame). It might feel like more than self-pity, your shame seems to affect every decision you make and define you as a person.

In order to break toxic shame, it's important to follow a series of helpful steps and reminders. First, repent of pride.[11] James 4 tells us that we need to submit and draw near to God. When we try to lift ourselves up to save ourselves, our prideful insecurities are reinforced when we fail. So, in defeat, we fall back down. Second, humble yourselves and accept help from the Lord. Don't give in to self-pity and shameful thoughts about yourself. Accept God's opinion of you and put your eyes on Him so that He can lift you up.

Don't seek introspection without first listening to the Lord; His true affirmations will come. We have to rely on and trust God's opinions and thoughts of us because our thoughts and opinions about ourselves are tainted. Renew your mind to change the way you think.[12] When we renew our minds, we are taking the old label, defining it, and changing it.

When you find yourself saying, *"I'm not good enough, I'm not worthy of love"*, replace those labels with God's word and truth. His Word says that there is no condemnation for those who are in Christ Jesus.[13] When you accept Jesus in your heart, you are no longer led by the flesh but by the Spirit. So, live it out! Your flesh is not in control, the Spirit is. Believe that the enemy and his lies don't have a hold on you any longer. Romans 8:14-16 says, *"For all who are led by the Spirit of God are sons of God. For you did not receive the spirit of slavery to fall back into fear, but you have received the Spirit of adoption as sons, by whom we cry 'Abba, Father!' The Spirit himself bears witness with our spirit that we are children of God…"* Receive the Spirit's revelation, affirmation, and love. Soak in His love day in and day out. Our foundation needs to be that we are worthy of the blood of His Son because the Father loves us. Slow down and bask in His presence. Listen to His voice and still your heart, He is right there with you, guiding you the whole way.

I had a lot of fluctuating feelings and ranges of emotions going through my mind throughout this inner healing process. It was bringing up a lot of past feelings that I had gotten pretty good at avoiding. Once it all came up in full force, it was hard to push back down. At times I would have a tough couple of days, feeling extremely depressed and alone. I wanted to be worthwhile and know that God saw me that way. I wanted to see what He saw in me. But that was still a hard concept for me to understand — that God viewed me as someone who could be valued by Him.

God was faithful to bring up difficult circumstances from my life, to force me to look back and realize He had answered prayers I didn't realize I had. When my mother was sick, God brought us closer to Him. When she was dying, we had a loving community around us. When she had passed, He gave me an incredible peace and an amazing family to call my own. When I struggled with depression and suicide, He was with me and drew me to Himself. The list goes on. He was showing me that He had been fulfilling promises in my past the whole time, and that His presence would always continue to be with me.

15 DEEPER DEVELOPMENT

Emotional and Spiritual Development

One of the hardest aspects of emotional and spiritual development, is going backwards to move forward. No one likes opening up old wounds and having to slowly take care of the hurts they've experienced in their past. Making the decision to experience inner healing is a long journey that in the end does result in understanding God's character and perspective on our life, rather than living with our own broken perspective.

In taking a trip back to my past, I had to analyze my developmental years to understand why my perspective on life was so broken. I knew I had some insecurities and really low self-esteem, but I never really understood why. Scazzero talks a lot about emotional and spiritual development in his book. He discusses unraveling your upbringing and identity, essentially what makes you who you are, and determining where emotional deprivation (emotional neglect that occurs in childhood or developmental years) may have occurred.

We all need to feel valued and safe (physically and emotionally), be able to give and receive love, and experience a sense of being understood, supported, and appreciated for who we are. When these essential components are lacking, our development suffers. We end up going through life lacking the essentials for emotional and spiritual health. We may think we are just insecure and have low self-esteem, but we are missing so much more. When our personal convictions, our passions, our image, our personality, and our character are damaged and unhealthy, our identity has been corrupted by the enemy. Until we are filled solely by understanding the character of God, we may struggle to find true healing. These essential components that encapsulate our identity all come from God. He is the essence of security, love, intimacy, acceptance, confidence, and significance. Through His character and image, we can have true emotional and spiritual health.

While processing my emotional health, it wasn't hard to find where I was lacking truth and love in my identity. I couldn't really remember when I first lost my self-confidence and self-esteem, but I always knew that I wasn't sure of myself and felt invisible around others. I constantly struggled with fully connecting with those around me, and it was difficult to accept affirmations from my friends because of my past insecurities and fears of abandonment. Everything relating to receiving and giving love from others felt like it was based on performance and achievements. Through this reflection, I understood that all I could really do was change the way I received affirmations and love from those around me.

The way I viewed love from my life experiences was that if I gave love and received it, I would lose it later on. I received love from my mother when she was sick, and then she died. I was close to my friends and then I moved away, so I felt like I lost their love too. This was a pattern that I was so used to and just accepted as a normal part of my life, which made it hard for me to truly connect with others. I knew I needed to start seeing those expressions of love as love from God, trusting that any relationship I had would be genuine and trustworthy because of Him. I needed to believe that any love I received in this world was placed in my life by God and founded on His love, not based solely on love from man. I didn't realize the hold those deprivations had on me, and that they had defined my behaviors and actions for so long. God needed to rewrite my story, redefine my identity in Him, and heal my heart so that my outlook on life would mirror His.

It is vitally important to determine where your emotional and spiritual maturity is on a developmental level, and where you need to grow in certain areas. Healing and growth will be more difficult if you can't address areas where you have been lacking in your past.

When you take the time to process your past and define where your childhood and development has been affected by neglect, it's important to embrace and listen to God's truth found in His Word. We desperately need truth from God and affirmations straight from Him. Create your own way of accepting His affirmations, because it is God speaking to you, the One who knows your heart even more than you do.

I have found that this kind of heart development and healing takes a lot of patience in processing the past. Once I discovered how my past had defined me, I could begin to modify my character to be in Christ. I used to always feel like I was missing something, like there was a hole I couldn't seem to fill. Sometimes without realizing it, our past hurts have impacted our soul so much that has left us with an incalculable and inconsolable emptiness that can only be filled by God's love. We must modify our character and how we view God to accept God's love completely. You can't trust someone until you truly know them, that includes God.

I encourage you to begin identifying the people that are available for you, the people you really trust to start modifying your character, because you can't do this alone. Be honest with them. Share your hurts and frustrations. If they take it upon themselves to show you how big the hole in your soul is, accept their help and guidance. There's nothing wrong with accepting help; you have to start somewhere to receive healing. We all need help in the beginning.

Once you are ready to face the emptiness, or hole, in your soul, go to God. Don't run from Him; the enemy will always try to make sure you feel like you're not enough and that you can't heal. In that moment, you need to call on someone else to help you. They can help you "set your mind on things above, not on things that are on earth."[14] You can navigate the healing process by surrounding yourself with the love of God and His truth. You are rebuilding the foundation of who you are by identifying your position in Christ.

Healing Deep Wounds

Everybody carries deep pain and hurt from being wounded, especially when it comes to analyzing our past; therefore, everyone needs healing from their wounds. Deep wounds usually affect our actions when we don't heal them, like an infection that isn't taken care of immediately and then infects the rest of the body. Analyze your overreactions and intense emotions to your surroundings and your circumstances. *What's underneath all of that?*

Isaiah 53 discusses how Jesus bears our pain.[15] God redeems the pain in our lives so that we can be like Jesus. He can redeem everything unfortunate that comes into your life. He does this by cultivating and growing our character into the character of Christ through our pain. James 1:4-5, says *"Count it all joy, my brothers, when you meet trials of various kinds, for you know that the testing of your faith produces steadfastness. And let steadfastness have its full effect, that you may be perfect and complete, lacking in nothing."*

In order to release control to God and allow Him to use our pain for His glory, we have to trust and believe that all things will actually work for His good. The work can't begin if we don't trust God to heal us first. Before you are ready to heal, you have to admit that you are in pain. Don't live in denial and don't ignore the wound. Let Him help you and give you His strength and love to seek and receive healing. He knows your heart, and He knows your pain. God even knows which root memories to address to help you heal from your wounds.

Once again, sometimes it takes going back to move forward. My friend Beth helped me understand this concept, and in a way, we did go back to the past to move forward in health. During my inner healing season, I knew I needed to address the fear and anger I held whenever I thought about my past with my mother and her cancer journey. I was so clouded by my hurt and frustration that all I could remember was fear, hurt, and anger. One night Beth asked me if I wanted to try this exercise with her. We would take some time to remember and rewrite my memories, with God being present in them. Since I had never done anything like this before, I knew I needed to trust that God was leading this exercise, and not me or Beth.

To start, Beth asked me to remember a time where I was the most scared and felt the most alone. The first memory I thought of was of me in a crib. I couldn't tell you why that was one of the memories, but Beth told me to picture God there in that memory, and to ask Him to help me to feel safe and loved. As I sat there, remembering and praying, I felt this peace. I felt sure that God had been with me and was loving me from the very beginning of my life.

We worked through another memory — when I was the most frightened I had ever been in my life. It was the night that my mother had multiple seizures while she was still sick with cancer. I still remember it vividly. But back then, I couldn't share that story at all with anyone. It was so paralyzing that I felt trapped in that memory every time I shared it because of the very real fear that was present there.

I've shared this story already, but the part that God wanted to rewrite for me was the part where I was waiting outside for the ambulance. Beth told me to imagine and really believe that God was there sitting on the sidewalk with me, waiting with me and comforting me. I really wanted God to rewrite that memory (and I knew that He could), so I prayed that the Holy Spirit would make that a reality for me. And He did. The memory was rewritten, and I was no longer afraid to remember that part of my story. You see, God was there too. And I believed that with all my heart.

———————————————————

It was so transformational to use the presence of Jesus to rewrite and heal those memories. After rewriting that story, I finally knew that in my darkest memory from my childhood, God was there with me. I could fully believe that He would never leave me. My eyes were opened to the root of my insecurities and my inability to fully connect with others. My fears of abandonment and loneliness brought on by my mother's illness and death somehow made sense. I could finally understand what God meant when He said that "He would never leave me nor forsake me."[16] I was confident that God is always with me, and He reminded me that I could trust in the people that He puts in my life. I didn't have to distance myself from others because of my fear of abandonment. Even if they leave or I leave, I'm never alone because God is always with me.

The Holy Spirit always shows the path of redemptive suffering through our memories. I encourage you to find someone to help you through this process if you have a difficult memory in your past, and journal about it so you can remember what God has done and how He has healed you. The process of redemptive suffering involves sitting and feeling the presence of God with your suffering sitting there too. Sit in silence, aware of His presence and aware of your pain. Sit in His presence with your pain so that He can expose the grief from within you and bring His light and joy to it. This will also bring light to the places that you have hidden deep inside of you, the places where you hold your innermost fears and desires. God will bring those to the surface and show you where He is in the midst of them. The healing process can be different for each person, and different every time, so follow promptings of the Spirit. Remember there are no quick fixes to healing; Jesus wants to walk with you through every step of this process.

After my summer in Spain, I slowly began to realize the work that God was doing in my life and in my heart. He was pushing me to experience more than my mind and imagination could fathom about His people and His purpose for my life. My trust in Him continued to grow, and my emotional and spiritual health was expanded. As I had traveled to different parts of Spain and learned about different ministries, my identity and worth became more solidified in Christ. I was becoming the person He always saw me as, but now I was able to discover that I had always been that person. His beloved child. My confidence in myself and in God grew. On a deeper and more intimate level I could see myself, my circumstances, and my past through God's perspective — and that changed everything for me.

All my worries and fears about other people's perceptions and opinions of me lessened. I started to understand what it meant to be an emotionally healthy and mature person the more that I changed right before my eyes. It wasn't an immediate change in my identity and self-worth, but a gradual one. I don't think I even knew the "exact" moment that I saw myself as a different and more whole person. As time passed, I began to love and value myself as God loves and values His children. I was able to approach unknown scenarios with boldness and trust that God was going before me. Each morning I started my day with God, releasing all my worries to Him and believing that He had the day planned for me. I just had to walk in it. Once I could see myself and my circumstances with God's view, everything looked more clear and more hopeful. But there was still work to be done.

16 WHEN YOU CAN'T MAKE SENSE OF YOUR OWN GRIEF

Grief. Grief is such a heavy topic to unravel. When it came time to address and learn about my grief, I was so reluctant. I still hadn't come to terms with any of my loss, because at this point, I had spent almost ten years avoiding it. For me, grief was like a never-ending season of trying to survive and thrive outside of a dark period of my life.

I couldn't bear to come to terms with my grief or accept it as anything other than a painful reminder that my mother was gone. I found myself, for a lot of my life, not understanding how I could be optimistic and hopeful when my life didn't seem to have much hope left. My reality quickly turned me into a pessimist because it was so hard to keep hope alive and believe that my life had any purpose left. I spent most of my teenage years depressed because I had given up on ever finding the happiness that I thought life could offer me.

But I was determined to find hope again though this inner healing process. I was tired of living in my own misery, and I wanted my life to look different. Knowing God meant believing that joy and hope existed, and I wanted to trust that His joy and hope could exist in my life too. But first, I had to be honest about where I was in my grief journey and where I wanted to be — from a dark place of hopelessness to a place where light unmistakably shined through. I knew lament was the first place to start.

Scazzero mentions the life of Job in his chapter on grief. He emphasizes the importance of lamenting to God and really expressing your anger and frustration and sadness. We need to "process before God the very feelings that make us human."[17] I didn't fully understand that at first. I was so used to holding my feelings in and refusing to show my anger to God. I didn't think He wanted to hear any of it.

But I was wrong, that's exactly what He wanted to hear from me. I needed to know that it was okay to yell, scream, and cry at God; it was okay to tell Him how I really felt about my loss. Only then could I deepen my relationship with God and really let Him into my grief. If I didn't express my raw and honest feelings to Him, then I wasn't being authentic and true in my relationship with Him at all. I was only denying myself true intimacy with my Father if I refused to show Him my anger, frustration, and sadness. Once I did, it was incredibly freeing to talk to Him openly about how I was feeling. It was truly beautiful and redemptive to be able to bare my broken soul to Him and have Him listen and love me more than I could have ever imagined was possible.

Lament also encourages us to embrace the uncertainty of grief when we can't understand what God is doing in our life. Grief brings confusion and mystery, and that's okay. It reminds us that we are not all-powerful or invincible. We can't know everything, only God can. Not having the full knowledge of what God knows and not having the answer to the question "why?" forces us to fully trust Him in all things. We don't need to know why, we just need to know that God is going to be there to comfort us and strengthen us, and He will. He did that for me and continues to do that for me. His presence is alive and constant. I can rest in that and not be plagued by the unknowns. I just have to submit those unknowns to Him and let go. "(Grief) humbles us like little else."[18]

In times of grief, we also need people to surround us. The power of community is what carries you and helps you gain perspective. You cannot go through grief alone. Asking for help is one of the hardest things we have to do in our grief. Being vulnerable and admitting that you are weak is not easy, but it is vital to live in this world. First, admit to God that you need help. Then ask Him to help you ask your brothers and sisters in Christ to come alongside you. We need people who are with us and for us when we don't have the strength to pick ourselves up. They remind us of the steadfast and present nature of our God and draw us back to Him time and time again.

Lastly, you need to spend time alone in silence and in solitude with God. When you've given yourself time to just be with God and with yourself, you can remember that He redeems all circumstances. Redeeming your loss and your pain doesn't mean God wants to gloss over your struggles and your grief; He doesn't want to help you get over it and tie it up with a nice bow on top. He wants to open your eyes and your heart to see His perspective on your loss, your pain, your grief, and your struggles. Take the time to seek the Lord's perspective on your circumstance and accept His comfort and encouragement. Ask Him how He will redeem this pain and loss, knowing and resting in the fact that He will either give you an answer or He will give you peace in the unknown. But trust that He will still redeem it.

Hold onto the unwavering truth of Christ and the power of His Word to find lasting peace and hope. Ask your friends and family for scriptures to remind you of His love and truth when you are too weary to search for yourself. Remember how He brought you through past experiences, so that you can recall His faithfulness. Your unwavering trust in Him will help you through your current struggle. Be strong in the Lord and rely on His power, not on your own, to get through each day of grieving.

God will always redeem the loss, no matter what kind it is. But you need to allow yourself to take the time to grieve that loss. Remember the people in your life that are there and *ASK FOR HELP*. Trust me, asking for help is the hardest part. But as time passes, you will find how to live with your grief instead of avoiding it. God is right there beside you, holding your hand, the whole time.

How Do You Keep on Grieving?

Knowing where to start in your grief journey is one thing. But how do you let yourself grieve daily? There are several practices that worked for me, especially when I was first opening myself up to my grief. These may or may not work for you, but it's important to find your own rhythm and safe place to grieve. For me, I would spend a lot of time journaling about my grief. This allowed me to get out of my own head and put the words and feelings I had on paper. I could be honest with God in my prayers, as well as in my journal. No matter what, God knew my heart so I knew I could trust Him with my feelings, the ones I understood and the ones I didn't. It was also helpful to pray the Psalms in my own words. I would read a chapter that related to exactly how I felt in that moment, then write a prayer like the Psalms or pray it out loud. I could express myself with words found in Scripture when I didn't have the words myself.

Letting myself feel free to express my grief didn't happen effortlessly. At times I still found myself mad at God, wanting to quit the work of healing every day. But that is part of lament. I couldn't repress it anymore, I had to let it out. It used to be easy for me to tell myself that I couldn't grieve, because I didn't want to feel the pain and it hurt too much. But not dealing with it, hurt even more. If I didn't allow myself to first be in pain to heal, any reminder or thought of my loss was going to continue to hurt and keep me stuck in a dark cycle of self-pity, hopelessness, and defeat. That is not how God desired for me to live my life, and it is not how I should've resigned myself to living. I was made for more, and it was time for me to start believing that for myself.

What I didn't realize before was that I needed to let myself feel the pain of grief every time I remembered my loss, because there would come a day when my grief didn't bring pain, but joy. Actual inexpressible joy that only comes from the Lord. I just needed to be patient and let my emotions out when they came to the surface. I needed to start embracing lament and letting myself feel the weight of all that had happened and all that I had lost. Only then, could I hope to move on and receive true healing.

Give God your pain, let Him take it all on. When you finally allow yourself to feel the weight of your grief, draw to mind God's words of truth and His perspective on your loss and suffering. You can be honest and admit the reality in front of you. But you don't have to be negative. You can grieve the bad stuff, but don't lose sight of the good parts of your life. Hold onto the eternal perspective. God will have the final word. As 2nd Corinthians 4:17-18 says, "For this light momentary affliction is preparing for us an eternal weight of glory beyond all comparison, as we look not to the things that are seen but to the things that are unseen. For the things that are seen are transient, but the things that are unseen are eternal."

Continually offer up praises and hallelujahs when you feel like it, and especially when you don't. When you allow yourself to process your grief, you are submitting your fears and worries to God and fighting for His promises of eternity. All of this will pass away, and one day we will experience eternity with those who have already passed on.[19]

As I spent time processing through my grief and asking God why my mother had to die, I felt like for the first time He answered me. God brought to my mind many moments where I had this burning feeling in my heart, like my heart was being lit up. Anytime I talked with another person about their pain or loss, especially if their loss was like mine, I felt this passion, like my feelings of empathy were on fire inside of me. This fire of emotions allowed me to understand how God viewed that person's story and loss, so I could see the beauty that God brings from pain. I had always wondered what the significance was in those experiences I had; I used to think it was just a different kind of grief. But the more I thought and prayed about it, the more I realized that my story, the one God had written for my life, held significance for the kingdom of God. I had discovered that I could connect with others who had similar experiences to mine because I understood their pain and grief on a personal level. My pain and loss allowed me to understand His character and love for me on an even deeper, more intimate, and eternal level, bringing me so much closer to God. He was inviting me to be part of sharing His gospel with others as I shared my experience of loss with them, helping them to see the abundant love of Christ in their life that I could now truly see in mine.

God had helped me understand why He took my mother home with Him — so that I could be His vessel to His people. I went through the previous ten years embracing and running from my grief, so that I could understand how important it is for others to have someone to show them Jesus in the midst of their unbearable pain and sorrow. People need to see the joy of the Lord in their pain. God redeems our suffering and uses our story for His glory. *Are you at a place in your life where you can see how God has redeemed your suffering and your loss? How is He speaking to you and calling you to be used through your story?*

Through the years, I have found that grief doesn't ever really end; it just evolves as we go through life. The more we process and experience it, the more it changes… and us with it. It's a beautiful and brutal experience that I am growing more and more thankful for in each passing year.

17 HEALING AND REDEEMING
THE DEEPEST WOUNDS

Depression

During the last part of my inner healing journey, I began to learn more about the dark valleys of depression. Now, at this point, I didn't fully understand what depression was. Back in grade school, no one openly talked about it because I think no one really understood what it was either. So, after my mother died and I started to view my life as worthless and pointless, I assumed that I was just grieving. I didn't think I was depressed. Even when I was struggling with suicidal thoughts, I thought that was just another aspect of grief. But I was depressed. I didn't think anyone would understand the darkness and loneliness that surrounded me, so I kept all of my feelings and fears inside.

These days, we can talk about depression and learn about it more openly. It isn't as obscure and avoided in our world and within our communities. I love that. There shouldn't be any shame or judgment associated with depression and mental illness. Mental health is a vitally important topic to discuss and learn about. We all need take care of our mental health and support those who struggle daily. This world is broken, and sin regularly tears down our emotional and mental health.

Depression is defined by the Mayo Clinic as "a mood disorder that causes a persistent feeling of sadness and loss of interest; it affects how you feel, think, and behave and can lead to a variety of emotional and physical problems. You may have trouble doing normal day-to-day activities, and sometimes you may feel as if life isn't worth living. It's more than just a bout of the blues; depression isn't a weakness, and you can't simply "snap out" of it. When depression persists, you may struggle to get out of the "funk" or "down" state of being."[20]

The Bible doesn't shy away from depression; the Psalms are full of laments, of crying out to God in our distress and despair. Psalm 13 is a great passage to learn from and read when you're struggling with depression. So, let's break it down a little.

> *1 How long, O Lord? Will you forget me forever?*
> *How long will you hide your face from me?*
> *2 How long must I take counsel in my soul*
> *and have sorrow in my heart all the day?*
> *How long shall my enemy be exalted over me?*
>
> *3 Consider and answer me, O Lord my God;*
> *light up my eyes, lest I sleep the sleep of death,*
> *4 lest my enemy say, "I have prevailed over him,"*
> *lest my foes rejoice because I am shaken.*
>
> *5 But I have trusted in your steadfast love;*
> *my heart shall rejoice in your salvation.*
> *6 I will sing to the Lord,*
> *because he has dealt bountifully with me.*

Verse 1 is a cry filled with hope; "how long" signifies that there is a timeline of the suffering. It's different from asking God why. When we lament to God, we understand His character and know that our suffering will not last forever. We can ask Him how long, and hope for an end to our current suffering or distress. In my experience, God has never given me an exact answer to "how long", but He has called to mind scripture that assures me I will have peace and I will feel His presence with me in my suffering. He will give me the patience to endure it. God knows that you can endure through Him. Verse 2 allows us to lament suffering alone, and question whether our enemy will overcome us. But we know that the enemy will not overcome us or leave us, even though we feel defeated. John 16:33 reminds us that Jesus will overcome the world. In verses 3 and 4, we are reminded that we can freely talk to God about our uncertainty and fears. We want Him to give us hope. Lastly, in verses 5 and 6, we are drawn back to the truth of God that we know in our hearts.

We can trust Him and be glad because He has saved us. We remember His promises and faithfulness, therefore we can praise Him and fight another day with Him on our side.

In the quiet moments of our suffering, it is vital to remember that God is there with us, but so are our family, friends, and our community. The importance of community in combating depression cannot be understated. Find your people that you can trust to be vulnerable, afraid, and full of doubt with. It's okay if you have a hard time asking them for help.

If you have a friend who struggles with depression, remember that it might be hard for them to ask for help. If you are wondering whether you should reach out, reach out. Be persistent. They need that reminder that you are there for them. Be annoying. It'll force them to let you in when they can barely admit they need you at all. Gauge their level of hope. How defeated do they seem? How open are they to talking in that moment?

Take the initiative and approach the tough subjects with them; don't be afraid to be persistent and show you care about that person. Connect with them so that they are open to sharing their story. It may take some time, but they need to practice opening up to you about their struggles. There is a time and place for discussing exactly what's going on with them, and finding a solution, but "fixing it" is not always the goal. Honestly, most of the time, they just need you to be there for them.

Help them understand who Jesus is, His character and truth, and their identity in Christ. Don't try to fix your friend, but nurture, understand, and give compassion to them. Perspective really helps when starting to discuss why they are depressed, so if you have any personal experience to share then do that. Make sure they don't feel alone, they may already feel like they are the only person in the world who is going through this.

Deciding to help others by encouraging them can be beneficial to you and to the one who is suffering. Remember if you have or are struggling with depression, ask for help and seek counseling. God will bring people to you in the right time, and He will give you the confidence and wisdom to share whatever you are willing to bring forth. Healing is a daily sacrificial process, just start by trying to be open to receiving it.

How to Overcome Fear

God says "fear not" multiple times in the Bible; and I think that's because He knew we would need multiple reminders. God knew that battling fear would be a continuous fight. Fear dominates our lives because of the sin in this world, but God is fighting alongside us, and He will win. Step out in faith and trust in God — that He will redeem and heal the spaces where fear resides within you.

Fear driven by our isolated and broken view on life, especially on our own inadequacies, can have an especially strong hold on us. Our innermost fears are typically the ones that are connected to past wounds. They may come out when we try to defend ourselves and when we begin healing and redeeming past wounds. But your past wounds, and the fears they produce, do not define you. Past experiences full of hurts and trauma do not define you. Any sin from the past or present has no ground to condemn or shame you. Though I didn't grow up with a father figure as a child and have struggled with insecurity, shame, low self-confidence, depression, and suicidal thoughts, it doesn't mean that those experiences have made me who I am. I can still be redeemed and healed from it all. I can be freed from my fears and insecurities. Believing that truth was the first step to finding healing and redemption.

Healing starts when we admit the wounds we have that lead to fear. God will present you with opportunities to overcome your fears if you let Him in. Name your fears and bring them into the light. My innermost fears are the fear of being alone, the fear of abandonment, and the fear of failure. As a result of neglecting to address those fears over time, they grew into deeper fears of inadequacy and shame that consumed my identity.

After you name them, identify how you tend to react to your fears when they are triggered. Feeling alone and feeling a sense of abandonment made me feel depressed and full of shame. These feelings led me to further retreat from the people in my life and believe the lies of inadequacy that the enemy used against me. I thought I was protecting myself from getting hurt, but the enemy was using those fears to push me further away from God and away from the people around me. When you understand these triggers, go to God immediately and confess your fears and doubts. Lament and believe what God says about you, instead of believing the lies of the enemy.

When our circumstances seem to have more power over us than God, we need to spend more time pouring over God's truth in His Word.

Read through Psalm 46 a few times. Let the truth of who God is sink in. Don't pray fear-based prayers, pray faith-based prayers. If we doubt that God can overcome our fears, then how are we trusting Him and believing that He can help us heal? Pray, believing that God is *FOR YOU*. God promises peace when we surrender and trust Him; and peace will come when we believe that God's perfect love drives out all fear.[21] Pray for redemption over your fears, and not just protection from your fears.

The God of Peace (and the peace of God) will be with you and will follow you, believe that.[22] Surrender your fears and anxieties to God and be still. Remember the Lord's presence is always with you; fix your eyes on Him. When those fears feel the strongest, fight to keep your eyes on Him. Don't let the lies of the enemy have a foothold. Read Psalms 46 again!

When you feel too weak to seek scripture or don't have the words to pray, leave the worship music on. Worship always and worship with thanksgiving and praise, then you will have peace.[23] The Spirit will pray for you when you don't have the words.[24]

This is how you can receive redemptive healing from your fears through the power of Jesus. Let Him comfort you; don't let sin patterns comfort you. Take ten minutes away from everything and everyone and access His presence. Surrender and trust Him to bring you peace. Psalm 62:1 says, *"For God alone my soul waits in silence; from Him comes my salvation."* Sometimes all you can do is wait on God because you may not be able to always fix a problem in one sitting. Be patient and wait on Him to speak to you. He will, whether audibly, through His word, or through another person.

Forgiveness

One of the last lessons I was learning in my season of inner healing, was how to repent and forgive. I mentioned a few chapters back about my season of forgiveness and battle with shame. Though I tend to think that I have learned enough about how to love those who hurt us, there is always something more to learn when it comes to taking care of our relationships with other people. I still struggled with bitterness and anger in my heart towards people, whether it was from hurtful words exchanged or because someone hurt someone I cared about. I knew I still had a lot to repent and forgive.

A great mark of spiritual maturity is the ability to love your enemies. Ephesians 4 goes into depth on how we as Christians are to live our new lives in Christ, and how we are to build each other up. Through forgiveness, we can have freedom in Christ. As Ephesians 4:32 says, *"we can forgive because we remember that Christ forgave us."* Being continually reminded of the truth of our salvation, we can act in kindness, tenderheartedness, and forgiveness towards one another — just as Christ did for us. When we are not sure if we have the power to forgive someone who has sinned against us, we should be reminded that having faith to achieve what God calls us to do is not of our own doing. When Jesus is talking to his disciples in Luke 17:5 about forgiving your brother when he sins against you, He says, *"If you had faith like a grain of mustard seed, you could say to this mulberry tree, 'Be uprooted and planted in the sea.' And it would obey you."* And in Matthew 17:20, He also says, *"...if you have faith like a grain of mustard seed, you can move mountains... and nothing will be impossible for you."* We must have faith that God will help us overcome anything that He calls us to do, including forgiving others. Obey God and forgive. If you have any amount of faith, He will do the work through you.

When we decide to forgive another person, we release the expectation that justice will be served, or that the person will admit wrongdoing and change their ways. We forgive so that we can heal hearts, ours and theirs. We act in love and choose to go beyond superficial forgiveness (when we say that we forgive but our heart is still bitter). We choose to love that person, and hope that God blesses them no matter what. We forgive, leaving all matters in the past behind us. God will enact justice for us because He goes before us. Therefore, we can rest in His truth and love for His children — all of His children.

So again, why do we forgive? Because God has forgiven us. In the parable of the unforgiving servant in Matthew 18, Jesus is sharing a story of the servant whose debt was forgiven by his master. But when another servant owed him a debt, he was not quick to forgive that person. The master (symbolizing Jesus) finds the servant and tells him that he should have had mercy on the other servant because he (the master) had mercy on him.[25] We are responsible to forgive, and not hold resentment or bitterness in our hearts. We need to give the same mercy and forgiveness that we have received from God to others.

But how can we practice that forgiveness in our lives? We can remember God's grace by meditating on scripture, listening to worship music, and by journaling to remember God's grace and mercy that has been shown to us. Pray blessings on those who sin against you, *"...Love your enemies, do good to those who hate you, bless those who curse you, pray for those who abuse you..."[26]* If we obey God when He calls us to forgive, He will shape and grow our character in ways that we can't imagine achieving on our own. We will be able to do that which we thought was impossible, through God's work in us. When you can't imagine forgiving someone who has wronged you, God will provide the space in your heart to forgive that person. In doing so, He will also heal your heart to forgive yourself, so that you can be released from any shame or guilt that you may be feeling as well.

Look for an opportunity to be a blessing to the person who wronged you. See yourself as like your offender (put yourself in their shoes), this can give you compassion towards them. Their heart needs healing, whether you know their story or not. No matter how deep the pain, and no matter how long the offense lasted, forgive. And keep on forgiving. Don't harbor resentment in your heart.

Forgiveness is an act of will, you must choose to forgive someone (or yourself). It is a decision made only by you and can be achieved only through you, not the other person. Therefore, it is a gift when we can receive it from someone else. You can't earn forgiveness; it is given to you. We cannot earn the forgiveness that Christ gave to us when He died on the cross for our sins, it was His gift to us. Through repentance and a commitment to live a life not in slavery to sin, we are choosing to not repeat the wrongs done to us or to others, or the wrongs we may have done to ourselves. We are choosing to live a life in freedom and submission to God by following Him.

Forgiveness may feel like a long process with many layers, depending on the hurt that occurred. You may not get it right every time, and healing may not be immediate. But if we go into forgiveness looking for a shortcut to make it fast and painless, quick apologies will surely lead to sorrow. But intentionality, vulnerability, and deep listening can lead to healing, breakthrough, and redemption. Our God is redemptive, and through Him we can live lives of freedom being filled with the Spirit that He gave us.[27] We do not have to do it alone. Let God have access to your heart to heal your wounds, only He can redeem your hurt. Make the choice to let go and follow the steps that He lays out for you in Scripture.

Repentance

Repentance and forgiveness go together and are a never-ending aspect of our redemption in our relationship with God. Repentance involves changing the way we think about our sin to bring us closer to the fullness of God. Remember, *"do not conform to this world, but be transformed by the renewal of your mind."[28]* In order to live out your life in the freedom of the light of Christ shining through you, you have to embrace the continual journey of sanctification (the process of becoming holy and righteous by God's work in our lives). Living in this broken world means that we can never be perfect and blameless (without sin) until we are in heaven with God. Sin is in this world and it's a fight against the enemy every day. We have God on our side, and though He has cleansed us from our sins (past, present, and future), we have to be accountable to repent and seek forgiveness every time we sin. This is part of becoming a new creation in Him, acknowledging the continual healing and growth that comes with a new life in Christ. The path to sanctification and redemption is filled with walking in the light and asking the Holy Spirit for help every day.

Titus 2:11-14 says *"For the grace of God has appeared, bringing salvation for all people, training us to renounce ungodliness and worldly passions, and to live self-controlled, upright, and godly lives in the present age, waiting for our blessed hope, the appearing of the glory of our great God and Savior Jesus Christ, who gave Himself for us to redeem us from all lawlessness and to purify for himself a people for His own possession who are zealous for good works."*

When we put to death all the sinful desires of our flesh and become people of Christ who live righteous lives, we are seeking to learn how to live pure and holy for God. Though we are not pure and holy while on this earth, God teaches us to live wholesome and honorable lives, seeking to do good works and live by faith until we are with Jesus in heaven. That is our purpose on this earth, to live a life full of sanctification and redemption. It will not be easy, Jesus never promised us that, but He did promise that He will be with us forever. *"I have said these things to you, that in me you may have peace. In the world you will have tribulation. But take heart; I have overcome the world."[29]* This world will be difficult, but God has already fought and won our battles, He is for us and with us for all eternity.

It took a while before I understood how to truly repent and forgive myself, and others, for the wrongs done to me. I knew how to repent to God for things I had done to others, but since I never truly understood how to forgive myself for the sins I had committed, it was difficult for me to fully receive God's forgiveness and love for me. I may have understood it in my mind, but I didn't feel it in my heart.

If you find yourself struggling with repentance and forgiveness, like I often do, it may be because shame is keeping you from experiencing true forgiveness. I struggled to allow myself to receive true forgiveness from God, because deep down I didn't believe that I deserved it. I felt like everything I had believed about myself, and had done to myself and others, was beyond repair and redemption. What I didn't realize was that those thoughts were due to the work of shame in my life. God wasn't disappointed in me, like I thought He was. Shame told me that I didn't deserve love and forgiveness. Shame told me that I wasn't worth anything, and that I didn't have value or significance. God's voice doesn't condemn us like shame does. His words are of love, not of disappointment.

Don't let your soul get consumed with shame. It is so important to confess your sins and your shameful thoughts to your friends you; don't let your heart harden. Proverbs 4:23 says that *"from the heart flows the springs of life (paraphrased)."* Let the wisdom and love of God permeate your heart. We need to protect our heart, and make sure that only the truth of God is inside of us.

Trust God, He will show you what you need to confess. Let Him communicate His forgiveness in your heart. The presence of the Holy Spirit can help you experience the reality of forgiveness and true healing in your heart. God knows your heart, so you can trust Him with your repentance and trust that He truly forgives and heals you.

18 SEEING WITH NEW EYES

Fullness of the Spirit

After I had completed my inner healing journey and was noticing the change that had happened in my life during that year, I felt this all-surpassing wholeness in my heart. God had filled my soul and my heart with so much overflowing beauty. I felt His presence and His Spirit with me continuously. I wanted to shout my praise and thanksgiving to God from the rooftops.

When we live in the reality of His presence, our life changes and we will not be able to contain it. When you are filled with the Spirit, God will work and move in you to share His work with others. Where does the activity of Jesus in your life intercept the brokenness of the people around you? That is where you can be a witness. We are called to be bearers of His Spirit. As we live in the fullness of His Spirit, His light will be undeniable to those around us, and He will give us opportunities to share His love with others.

We need to be like Christ in all circumstances and display His love for us by doing what He would in every aspect of our lives. I have learned from in this inner healing experience that suffering gives us the opportunity to share the gospel in a unique way. We can always relate to the Word of God, and to the life of Jesus. So, let Him use you to spread the good news!

For the first time, I felt at peace with the entirety of my story. I knew that when suffering would inevitably knock on my door again, I would believe, have faith, and hope in God to sustain me when life's questions yielded little to no answers. My acceptance of suffering encouraged me to believe that in the face of uncertainty, I could rely on the truth of the gospel to give me peace. I didn't need to know why my story was written with loss, because I knew that God wanted me to proclaim who He is to others through my story of suffering. He wanted me to share with others why I believe what I believe, that is what I aspire to do every day of my life. And now, I love sharing my story with everyone He brings into my life.

When I'm around people who share a story similar to mine, it no longer pains me but fuels my heart. I can see the potential and need for sharing my story and the gospel. There's an indescribable joy that comes when I hear another's story and see what God has done, or has the potential to do, in their lives. My heart races just thinking about it. Whatever God chooses to do with my life, and through my suffering, all the glory will go to Him. The redemption and salvation of others makes all the pain and suffering I have gone through, and will go through, worth it.

Heaven-anniversary in Spain

Ten years after my mother died, my grief felt different for the first time. I knew that everything I went through all those years, had brought me to this point. The pain was still there, and I still missed her deeply, but now I didn't want to avoid feeling my grief. I didn't want to hide from everyone anymore.

I was processing my emotions differently now. I was no longer mad at my mother for dying and leaving me, or at God for taking her home. I wasn't depressed like I used to be, I just missed her immensely. I am thankful that my grief was healing me, and that I could accept and embrace it now. Celebrating her heaven-anniversary was actually a blessing this time. I could finally reflect and appreciate all that God had done and given to me since my mother had passed. What a gift!

Reflections from Spain

It was such a blessing being in Spain that year. In the beginning, I was so afraid to go, and I doubted that God was really sending me. I didn't want to leave my comfort zone in the U.S. with my family. But as my trip came to a close, I didn't regret a single moment that I spent in Spain.

Following God's call to an unknown adventure was one of the scariest decisions I had ever made, but it turned out to be one of the best ones. It was an amazing experience to see God change my perspective on life in ways I never imagined possible.

God led me to Spain when I had a reluctant but obeying heart, and by the end, I could clearly see that the benefits and blessings outweighed all the fears and worries I had. My experiences there, all of the amazing people I met, and all the various ministries I spent months learning about, allowed me to grow profoundly in the Lord. Deciding to step into inner healing gave me the push I needed to understand and embrace my past, so that I could fully comprehend who God is and who He created me to be. I left that country a completely different person, but someone God always saw me as. Now when I looked in the mirror, I saw the person He saw too.

I can say with utmost certainty that answering God's call and trusting Him to know what is best for you is the best decision that anyone can make. That beautiful feeling of unwavering certainty and trust in God, and His call and will for your life, is like no other. You may not believe it until you get the chance to experience it for yourself, so I pray that those of you reading will take that leap of faith into the unknown, but rewarding, life God has in store for all of us.

> *"What no eye has seen, no ear heard, nor the heart of man imagined, what God has prepared for those who love Him."*
> *(1 Corinthians 2:9)*

> *"And we know that for those who love God all things work together for good, for those who are called according to His purpose."*
> *(Romans 8:28)*

PART IV

19 LIFE IN MINISTRY

Once I returned to New York later that year, the only thing I was certain of after my time in Spain was that I wanted to pursue work in ministry. I had grown a passion for loving people and for serving them in any way that I could; and my heart for others and for God had grown abundantly. So, I came back wanting to learn more about what a life in ministry, specifically vocational ministry, looked like. Watching other missionaries live their lives out for the gospel was so inspiring to me, I wanted to learn how to do the same.

By December of 2016, I had moved back to Orlando, Florida and the search began to find a new job and a new home church. Within a few weeks, God opened up an opportunity for me to work at a long-term care facility in Winter Garden, so I relocated to the West Orlando area. A family friend heard from my parents that I was going to be working nearby and recommended that I try out Mosaic Church. I fell in love with Mosaic immediately, and by January I had settled into my new job and into my first apartment. I was nervous and excited, as a new season of adulthood was beginning, with so many new opportunities to look forward to.

Discovering Ministry

Though I had grown a passion for ministry, I wasn't quite sure where to start cultivating it. All I knew that I wanted to do in ministry was that I wanted to come alongside others as they grew in their faith and point them towards Jesus. Many of the young adult and student ministry staff at Mosaic could see my growing heart for ministry, so they all encouraged me to apply for the church internship where I could learn and grow this new passion.

But discouragement, quickly brought more stress to a new and exciting season of my life. Once I had begun the internship that fall, I still struggled to see the potential God, and others, saw in me even though He was continually equipping and empowering me to lead and disciple others. So, while I quickly felt like a career in ministry would be the next step after the internship, the fear of the unknown overwhelmed me. I knew it was entirely possible that working in ministry at Mosaic wouldn't be the exact next step that God was calling me towards after my internship. But the more I prayed about it, the more I felt like God was telling me to just trust that He would supply me with everything I needed to do what He was calling me to do.

Nothing ever happens in an instant when it comes to waiting on God's plan. He wasn't going to tell me in one day whether I was going in the right direction for my future or not. I'd have to take it one day at a time, as frustrating as that was to do. Everything happens in His time, not my own. I needed to be confident that God was still using me in every opportunity He set in front of me. I needed to enjoy what He was teaching me in each moment.

Throughout my internship, I was able to discover that God had given me specific spiritual gifts of mercy and service. I was grateful to be able to use them for His glory as I spent time serving with the young adult community and my high school small group each week. My passion for discipling others in their relationship with God grew, as my heart to care for their stories continued to grow as well. God had done so much for me, and I deeply desired to do the same for others.

As the months passed, I felt more confirmed that vocational ministry was where God was leading me, so I began praying for more direction in my life. But the worry returned once again. I began to worry whether my dreams and desires would even be fulfilled. I battled a lot of uncertainty and doubt, even though I knew to trust in God's will and plan for my life.

The enemy is a thief of joy and a master at making us question everything, but God teaches in His word that when worry increases within us, we need to look inward and allow God to work in us. Philippians 4:6 says, *"do not be anxious about anything, but in everything by prayer and supplication with thanksgiving let your requests be made known to God."*

James 1:2-3, says *"Count it all joy, my brothers, when you meet trials of various kinds, for you know that the testing of your faith produces steadfastness."* Our external trials force us to grow inwardly, further solidifying and strengthening our faith. I was still learning that the redemptive work God does within us is never done. In order to care for our souls, we need to invite God's love to surround us and bring us back to the journey of redemption. His love is what brings us out of the depths of darkness over and over again. He never lets us go or gives up on us when we feel discouraged, exhausted, or unmotivated. He is in every moment, the good, bad, the boring, the exciting, all of it.

When God is leading us into redemption, it takes work to change the inner habits of our minds and thoughts, especially when we are struggling with worry and doubt. We were never capable of providing ourselves with certainty and joy, and that's okay. God does that for us. He supplies everything we need because He loves us. We are constantly trying to do things on our own, but we only need to ask God and He will provide exactly what we need to take that next step into an abundant and joy-filled life.

Most of the worry in my life has come from a struggle to keep trusting God. The full life, the one overflowing with joy and peace, happens only as I come to trust in Him fully. When we are not troubled or anxious about the stresses of this world because we have cast all our cares upon Jesus, we can relax, trust, and lean into His dependable arms. He never burdens His children with shame or self-condemnation when our trust in Him falters, instead He calms our fears with His gentle grace. We have to keep trusting in Him every day, reminding ourselves of His faithfulness and love displayed throughout our lives.

Don't Worry, Be Happy

As I was getting used to a new rhythm of living, working, and doing life in a new town, I found a lot of solace and comfort in going to beach as often as I could. In the past, God always used that time to speak to me and encourage me as I brought my concerns, worries, and frustrations to Him. It was so important for me to find a place that brought me complete peace and allowed me to empty my mind, so that God could fill it with His words of affirmation, confirmation, and love. All my worries, fears, and anxieties completely melted away when I was in God's presence at the beach. The beach has always been a place just for me to be myself with Him.

During my times at the beach, God would often remind me of the importance of embracing my present life instead of worrying about the future. God calls each of us to enjoy the life in front of us. It's hard to live carefree in this world, where the lifestyle and motivation for life is found in the work you do. When we learn how to bring our worries and fears about the future to God, He will remind us that everything we need to know to prepare and live well, is found in Him.

We tend to have big dreams, we work every day and night, and we have numerous ideas running through our minds. So, it's easy to tell God how we think life should be. Instead, listen and trust Him. *"Here's what I've decided is the best way to live: take care of yourself, have a good time, and make the most of whatever job you have for as long as God gives you life."* Ecclesiastes 5:18-20 the Message version continues to say, *"We should make the most of what God gives, both the bounty and the capacity to enjoy it, accepting what's given and delighting in the work."* When we are occupied with cheerful and grateful hearts because of what God has done in our lives, we don't have time to worry or dwell on the days ahead, because we are satisfied with what He provides now. With this mindset, we can live our lives full of contentment and joy.

As we will inevitably have good and bad days in this life, God calls us to embrace them both. When we embrace pain, grief, and our seasons of suffering, God is inviting us to grow in maturity and wisdom. The pain forces us to confront the inner workings of our heart and soul. We can't reach those depths without God, and only He can save us when we feel defeated and overwhelmed. Ecclesiastes 7 reminds us, *"... in your good days, enjoy them. Live life to the fullest; take advantage of what that day has to offer. On bad days, be intentional about invading your soul and conscience. Embrace harsh realities and watch spiritual growth and maturity emerge. To be a person who fears God, you have to learn to deal with the responsibility of all of reality, not just a piece of it."* Embrace God's gifts in every season.

I've learned to be thankful for the hard days when it seems like nothing in life makes sense. I can trust that those days will produce wisdom within me. I find that on the days where I am confused and burdened, I am more motivated to seek understanding and knowledge from God. He doesn't always give me the answer I am seeking, but I grow closer to Him in the midst of seeking His truth and wisdom for my life. Wisdom from the Lord has to be grown, nourished, and refined through consistently studying His Word, especially in hard times.

In the midst of seemingly unreasonable suffering, there exists patience in suffering, joy in suffering, hope in suffering, and, again, joy in suffering. We have to embrace joy when it comes our way. We can't let despair, fear, and anxiety win over our hearts. God loves us too much to keep us where we are.[30] He allows us to suffer to cultivate growth and character, but remember the pain will not last forever. He's growing us because He loves us. Remember that in your suffering.

On any given day, this world can get so overwhelming that it can paralyze you, physically, emotionally, and spiritually. Rest in Him. Silence and solitude may seem like an impossible feat, but the beauty and peace of Christ is so worth it. Let God wrap you in His arms today, quiet your soul and your heart, and whisper words of affirmation and love that were meant just for you. His love for you doesn't fail, doesn't judge, and doesn't make you feel inadequate, insignificant, or alone. He sacrificed His Son on the cross because of His love for us. And why? Because we are His children, and always have been. You are His child, and He loves you.

Even when you don't feel confident and effective in what God has done through you, He will still use you. Don't run from the pain of redemption and growth as you mature in Christ. The hard things we face on this planet are refining us. Don't avoid them. God is waiting to walk you through it. Trust me, the journey is worth it.

Shame's Deception

Though I had learned and healed a lot while I was in Spain, worrying about my future quickly brought back feelings of inadequacy and more insecurities into my mind. It felt like I had gone backwards in my healing; I felt like I had failed. But God didn't view me as a failure. He sees the redemption and healing process as beautiful, and He will not let shame defeat us.

During my internship with Mosaic, I had the opportunity to hear Curt Thompson speak about shame and discuss some of the topics he unravels in his book, *The Soul of Shame*. He shared a lot of insightful thoughts about how entering the process of sanctification and redemption can also mean dealing with our shame. Though shame threatens to tear apart what God has grown within us, God uses our struggle with shame to bring truth about His love for us to the surface so that we can heal from our past. But it's a hard journey. As the mind is refining itself from past hurts or trauma, it goes back and forth between entering a cloud of shame to entering a clear sky of God's recognized love.

Curt Thompson explains that the mind is an embodied and relational process that emerges in and within the brain, whose task is to regulate information. The mind works together with our entire body, and it cannot function on its own, it needs interaction with another mind. In his discussion, he explained that since the mind is always moving, when we experience shame, our mind is limited in its movement. For example, when you experience shame because of something you did, or because of something that was done to you, it can be difficult to process that information. When we struggle to process that event in our mind, we may retreat from others because we don't want them to know our shame. But in order to heal, we need to have people in our lives who are willing to ask us the tough questions that will encourage us to be known. Ask yourself, *why is it so hard for you to let yourself be known by others? Do you truly believe that people won't stick around if they know the real you?*

As soon as shame enters in, condemnation surfaces. It's the first verbal language of how you are feeling in your shame; the harbinger of abandonment. We were made to be vulnerable and without shame. But when condemnation is in play, we isolate and limit ourselves from bringing others into our lives because of our shame and the fear of what they will think about us. Shame depends on isolation to be effective. The most damage happens in the privacy of our own mind. Evil uses shame not just to hurt you, but to destroy you, so that you are no longer able to do what you were created to do — which is live with God in community.

Suffering becomes more prolonged when it isolates and condemns. But Hebrews 12:1-2 reminds us that the race is set before us. God has already gone before us and defeated the enemy. Fix your eyes on Jesus. Imagine He is looking at you with an expression of love, unconditional love, before, during, and after you sin and feel shame. He knows your heart, and He isn't going anywhere. Why is it hard to believe that the Father, Son, and Spirit is always with you and is excited to be with you? Because shame tells us through several lies from the enemy that this is not true. Shame is the liar. God is the truth.

See Jesus in the eyes of others when they come alongside you and be like Him when others ask you to come alongside them. We need to look at Jesus and each other and be reminded of His truth, to renew those areas of shame. Sanctification happens when we are viewing ourselves in light of

God's mercy. When we start to do this in regularity, we will begin to view ourselves rightly (not lower or higher than God intended), thus creating a renewed mind.

Another way to combat the shame that enters your mind is to be in constant communion with God. When we are praying and talking with Him about everything that is going on, we will be able to rely on Him more readily. When shame threatens to consume your mind, bring scripture to mind and God will give you peace. Trust that He will take care of you as He has before and will continue to do.

Where is Your Ministry?

As my internship was coming to a close the following spring of 2018, I knew that I wanted to pursue vocational ministry at Mosaic, but no opportunities were available yet. God had other plans first. He needed to show me that ministry was not dependent on whether I worked at Mosaic, and it was not limited to Mosaic. Ministry is in the everyday and all around us. I needed God to help me see that ministry was in every opportunity in front of me, at the nursing home I worked at, in the grocery store, with my family and friends, everywhere. We can share and be the gospel everywhere.

We need to be thankful for the ministry we are in, whatever it looks like. In every encounter you have with a person, view every man in the light of God. He gives us the light of the gospel in the darkest places.[31] Our main purpose on earth is to be the light. So, we should pray that the light of Christ in our hearts will shine in the midst of the darkness of this world.

Christ is our strength when we feel weak because we have the power of Christ within us, the same power that raised Him from the dead. The apostle Paul reminds us in 2nd Corinthians that the power that raised Jesus from the dead lives in us. The power of His sacrifice and His love was displayed on the cross, so that His life could be revealed through us. Jesus's sacrifice, death, and resurrection emphasizes the power of His life over death. His light is at work in us so that others may see the light of His gospel in God's own timing. We are going through death (Christ's death) and suffering so that others can experience life, so do not lose heart!

Even though outwardly we are wasting away, and inwardly it may feel like we are wasting away, God is doing amazing work within us. Inwardly we are being renewed every single day. As we receive the fruit of the work of the Holy Spirit and the power of Christ in our lives, our hearts and minds are being renewed. *"Our light and momentary troubles are achieving for us an eternal glory that far outweighs them all. Hold fast to that! Don't lose heart or give up hope. Eternal glory is coming! We fix our eyes not on what is seen but on what is unseen. For what is seen is temporary, but what is unseen is eternal."*[32] Do not lose hope in the eternal. Hold fast to the promises of God, and He will guide your next steps.

During the year and a half that I was back in Florida, God had been working within me to trust in His truth, His promises, and His love for my future. And I was going to need to remember all that He had taught me as I stepped into this next season of my life.

20 WHEN MY WORLD STOPPED MOVING

On Memorial Day the summer of 2018, I was on my way to work when my phone rang. It was my mom, Nancy, calling. When I answered, she said three words I would never forget. "Dad is gone." I wasn't sure I had heard her right, so I told her to repeat herself. She said that my dad (Orlando) was gone. He was with Jesus now. I still didn't understand, my dad couldn't have been gone. I just talked to him the other day; he was supposed to be heading to New York for work. My mom told me to pull over and asked if I could come to the house. My head and my heart were pounding in disbelief, I was in shock… my dad was dead?

Reality started to sink in, and I started to hyperventilate. So, I pulled over into a nearby neighborhood. I told my mom I would call into work and let them know I couldn't come in, and head straight to her house. I got off the phone with her, and texted my supervisor at the nursing home saying there was a family emergency and that I wouldn't be able to come in. I couldn't manage to say out loud, or even text, the words that my dad had died. There was no way this was real, right? But my mom wouldn't lie about something like that, I could hear it in her voice. As I was coming to the realization that I would have to drive to Orlando in a minute, I knew I needed to collect myself first. So, while I was parked in front of some stranger's house, I let myself sob deeply for a few seconds, and then tried to calm myself down. A woman heading to her car, saw me parked outside of her house and came to my door. She asked if I was okay. I told her, *"No, my dad just died."* She asked if she could pray for me, and I knew in that moment that God was right there with me.

After the kind woman left, I headed to my parents' house. Well, now I guess it was just my mom's house. I was still trying to process everything and come to terms with the fact that my dad was actually gone, but I couldn't seem to make sense of any of it. Then a thought came to mind, my worst fear had been realized. After my mother died, in the back of my mind, I knew that if I ever lost another parent, that would be my biggest fear and I told myself I wouldn't be able to survive it. I had forgotten that was my worst fear, and it had just happened. I did lose another parent. I thought that I wouldn't experience anything like this again, and I did. That reality hit me like a ton of bricks. It had happened, and, for a moment, I knew I was going to be okay.

Once I got to my mom's house, we hugged each other and cried in each other's arms. My mom continued to call family and friends to let them know about my dad. I can't remember if my mom told me what had happened on the phone, but I got more details when I reached the house. My dad did head out early that morning to drive to New York, but was hit by a car that was driving on the wrong side of the road on the highway. It was a head on collision and my dad had died instantly. The other driver was rushed to the hospital and was still in critical condition. I was in disbelief that he was gone so quickly, I just couldn't believe it.

The calls and texts from people at church, people at work, friends, and family started to flood in. But I didn't respond. I couldn't believe it and I wasn't ready to come to terms with any of it. Some people called me directly, and I barely heard their condolences. I thanked them, accepted their prayers, and said goodbye. I talked with my siblings, who were struggling, mourning, and inconsolable. My mom wasn't okay, but she was handling everything well and kept us all taken care of. Family and a couple of friends came by the house to check in and bring food. We all cried so much, tried to eat, and attempted to make it through day one.

When I finally got back to my place later that night, my brain couldn't comprehend what had happened that day. The disbelief honestly lasted for the rest of the year and even into the next year. No one tells you that when someone dies instantly, your brain can't understand a loss that immediate. It doesn't make sense that someone who existed in your life is no longer there anymore. My dad traveled for work often, which only made it harder to tell myself that his absence was permanent this time. My brain just kept telling me that he was away for work, and that was why he wasn't around. But the circumstances around me kept forcing reality to tell me different. In the beginning, the most difficult part of my grief was trying to make sense of the fact that my mind couldn't catch up with reality.

That first night I, reluctantly, found the grief journal that I had started back in Spain, and wrote this entry:

"Dad died today. On Memorial Day. May 28, 2018. It still doesn't seem real. The whole day I felt like, and still feel like, I'm experiencing someone else's father dying. Like it's someone I know. And not me. Not sure when it will all hit me. But I need to make sure I'm not alone when that happens. Still doesn't feel real at all."

I barely slept that night, I felt so sick to my stomach. Everything was still so surreal, and I was overwhelmed thinking about going to Mosaic the next day to see people and experience their kindness and condolences. But they were also my family, so I knew I needed to let them be there for me. I had more people in my corner at Mosaic than I realized who had experienced this kind of loss. And that was an odd comfort.

During that first week, the anger of grief began to slowly burn inside of me. I'd be spending time with my family, and all of a sudden, I would get frustrated with everyone. I was just so tired of talking and thinking about my dad's death. After leaving my family each day, I would go spend time with my friends, and they would tell me how much my dad loved me and how proud of me he was. They would encourage me to try and think about all the things my dad would say to me. But immediately, tears would overflow on my face because the only person I wanted to talk to about everything that was going on was my dad. I wanted to talk to him about the wild fact that he was dead. I wanted him to comfort me, but he was the one who was gone.

Throughout each day, my brain would just cease to work, and I'd exist in this fog. I couldn't seem to comfort myself. Others came through on that, but it didn't change the fact that I didn't want this to be my life anymore. I felt so defeated when it came to thinking about my life because my story was once again filled with tragedy and loss. I didn't want this reality to be mine.

My dad's death confused me a lot more than my mother's death did. For weeks it didn't feel real at all. And I wasn't sure if it was because I was avoiding the grief, or if it was because it hadn't sunk in yet. I didn't want it to sink in, but I also didn't want to avoid feeling it like I had in the past.

I spent a lot of time reflecting on how my grief was playing itself out this time. My dad had brought me through the loss of my mother, so because of that I knew that I could find a way to get through his death. I knew some days would be harder than others, and I knew that I would feel it more in some moments than in others. Some nights I had to tell myself over and over again that, in my heart, I knew he was gone, even if I didn't feel it yet. I knew that he was with the Lord. My dad was the closest example of Christ in my life, and that gave my mom and I hope and confidence that we would be okay. We had the hope of the Lord and the hope of eternity to keep us going. Our grief wouldn't look like the world's grief, and the Holy Spirit would guide us along the way. We had to cling to that truth in those early days of grief.

The day before my dad's celebration of life service, I went to the beach to spend some time with God. I knew that I needed a familiar place to just sit and mourn with Him, and the beach had always provided that for me. I could let myself feel everything, and for the first time I missed both my mother and my dad with the deepest longing and sorrow I had ever felt.

The next day I would have to say goodbye to my dad with the rest of my family, friends, and his worldwide community. It was an overwhelming thought, and it immediately made everything all too real. I hadn't wanted to see his body, read the news, or come to terms with any of it before I was ready. But I knew that I had to be. I didn't want him to be gone, but he was.

In those moments on the beach, there was so much that I was beginning to realize I had lost when my dad died. He wouldn't get to walk me down the aisle, hold my kids and get to know them, tell me any more jokes, give me wisdom, share words of encouragement, or hug me anymore. All I had left were my memories of him, and I desperately wanted to be able to keep him alive in my heart, like my mother was. It felt like too much to bear knowing that I had lost so much when he died. I had no choice but to trust that I would be okay with God's presence and love to sustain me.

The day of the celebration of life service was one of the hardest days of my life. It was so much more public than I had imagined it would be. But my dad had also impacted so many people in his life. Mourning with the world was an interesting experience, very vulnerable but sweet. I'm so thankful we could celebrate and honor him in the way that we did. I'll never forget that day for the rest of my life. Though my anxiety and grief felt overwhelming, God brought scripture to me through other people, so that I could be reminded that He is sovereign and an ever-present help in all things.

> *"The Lord will not grow tired or weary, He gives strength to the weary and increases the power of the weak. Those who put their hope in the Lord will renew their strength. They will soar on wings like eagles; they will run and not grow weary; they will walk and not faint."*
> He is our Hope. (Isaiah 40:28-3)

> *"And we know that in all things God works for the good of those who love Him." "If God is for us, who can be against us? He didn't spare His own song but gave him up for us. He will also graciously give us all things."*
> He is for us. No one and nothing shall separate us from the love of Christ. We are more than conquerors through Him who loves us. (Romans 8:31-39)

> *"He is our refuge and strength. He is ever-present. He dwells in the holy place. God is within us, we will not fall. God will help us. He lifts His powerful voice. He is with us. He is our fortress. His works are magnificent and majestic. Know He is God. Be still. He is and will be exalted. He is with us. He is our fortress."* (Psalm 46)

> *"Rejoice in the Lord. Be joyful in God your Saviour. When the world around you tells you to give up, rejoice and be glad."The sovereign Lord is my strength. He makes my feet like the feet of a deer (light of burdens). He enables me to go on the heights."*
> We can do all things through Him who gives us strength and makes our burdens light. (Habbakuk 3:17-19)

As the weeks after the celebration of life progressed, people continued to express their amazement at how positive and at peace with everything I seemed to be. I knew that grief was different for me this time. I was in a much healthier place with my emotions because my hope was in the Lord and my trust in Him had grown deeper. I was willing to let myself feel and process my grief instead of avoiding it, no matter how hard it would be.

Any time I felt like my emotions were close to overwhelming me, where all I wanted to do was retreat and run away from life, God would comfort me before I could give any of my anxiety a second thought. God's promises in His Word made so much more sense than anything else around me. He was the only reason I could make it through each day.

His promises are stronger than anything. Only God can provide peace that surpasses all understanding. We can get through tomorrow, the next day, and forever because of Him.

Life Forever Changed

As life continued to move forward, I found myself analyzing and processing how my life and the lives of those around me were different since my dad was gone. My grief seemed more mature this time around, so I couldn't help but allow myself to take the time and try to understand it as best I could.

After my dad died, I started to let myself dwell on the fact that some things would never be the same again. For example, before, if I ever had a big decision to make, I would talk it through with him before I did anything, because I trusted his opinion and appreciated his thought process. But without him in my life anymore, who would I talk about big decisions? It constantly blew my mind that even how I would continue to grow and change throughout my life would be different, because my main confidant was no longer there to guide me. It even felt wrong to go to work and just resume normal life.

When tragedy happens and halts the normal rhythm of life, it's harder than you think to move one foot in front of the other. You may find yourself feeling anxious, wishing you weren't even having to go through the motions of life at all. You may feel like everything is still happening all over again when people tell you that they are sorry for your loss. Maybe you can't seem to do your work and focus properly anymore. You might even realize that you have to work more slowly and meticulously, because performing normal functions that you used to do are harder. As time passes, this new part of life, "after death", can feel really discouraging. But you have to be honest with yourself about how you are feeling, in order to move forward and process your loss.

My dad was such a huge part of my life, so I felt the huge void that he left in my life when he died. This time I wanted to fill that empty void in a healthy way. God seemed like an easy answer, but that empty feeling still kept coming back, reminding me that a part of my heart was gone. The emptiness didn't always hurt when I felt it, but the void was still there. Feeling that empty, dark void is what made me not want to do anything, not even smile or talk. But I knew that I couldn't remain in that state of being. I needed to have patience and grace for myself in those moments. My church community and close friends kept reminding me to have grace and patience for myself when I didn't have the strength to do it. They showed me so much love during that hard season, and I'll be forever grateful to them for that.

At some point after loss, you will have to attend the first event or activity that you would have done with the person who has died. Not even two weeks after my dad died, I was headed to a wedding in New York that we were supposed to have attended together. We had made plans to have a much-needed father-daughter trip. I recall feeling really overwhelmed because everything seemed to be reminding me that my father was gone. It was like the world was telling me that he didn't exist anymore, that the person who was my dad was completely erased from my life. I knew that wasn't true, but it was difficult to be constantly reminded that he wasn't there when he should have been.

I was glad to be with some of my family at this wedding as the event brought me momentary joy, but also lasting pain. I couldn't help but think about how a lot of the tangible ways a mother and father are represented on earth are seen and experienced. My mom Nancy embodied some of the void that my mother Darlene left when she passed, and then other mother figures helped to fill that emptiness. But there was no father figure to fill my dad's place. All of the dances at the wedding would remind me of the somber fact that I would never dance with my dad at my own wedding. He would never walk me down the aisle or give me away, or even officiate my wedding like I always imagined he would.

All the father responsibilities I would miss out on just kept flooding through my mind. The intense sadness and grief I felt made me want to run away from everything. Grief early on made me feel extremely lost and defeated. Somehow, I still had peace, which I knew only came from God, but I felt really lost.

On my first Father's Day without my dad, I was going to write him a letter, but this is all that I could manage to write in my journal:

I don't know what to say to you dad. Except that I love you and miss you so much. You have always been my person. My counsel and go to guy. I told you nearly everything about life. You got me excited about ministry and Spain. Life didn't seem real until I told you about things. So, thank you for that. Thank you for inspiring passion in my heart. A love for others. For strengthening my trust in the Lord to go after what God calls me to do. Thank you for never giving up on me and always going the extra mile and pushing me so far, all the time. I'm brave because you encouraged me to be. Life doesn't seem like life without you. It's hard to make the next step without seeking your counsel. I love you so much and I thank God for placing us together every day. You mean the world to me. so much. Love you dad. Miss you. - Love with all of my heart, Meena

God's Work Isn't Done

A couple weeks after my dad died, and after I had completed my internship at Mosaic, I jumped back in to serving the young adult and student ministries. But deep down, I didn't feel like I could serve in ministry the same way as before. I still wanted to be present and serve at church, even though I was feeling ineffective and like a burden to others while in my grief. I felt drained and empty, lacking the passion I had just discovered weeks before my dad had passed. Everything I was excited and passionate about in my internship had faded completely. It felt like I had no passion, drive, or purpose anymore. I couldn't figure out how to function the same. My strength was gone, but I had faith that God would provide everything I needed to be present and follow His will for my life in ministry one day at a time.

One day God brought to my mind Colossians 1 where the apostle Paul is explaining how God is *"before all things, and in Him all things hold together."*[33] He is the beginning of everything. Before we were made, He was there. He holds everything together, so He holds us together. He holds our circumstances and our lives together despite what's going on around us. He is our hope, our strength, and our power when we have none. He gives us endurance and patience when we have none. I needed these reminders to help me get through each day, one day at a time.

As far as finding my purpose again, I was reminded that God's will for me wasn't something I would do tomorrow, but about everything I would do in each day in front of me. Everything you are doing right now is fulfilling God's will. Do what He has called you to do right now, because it will reflect how you live the rest of your life. God's purpose and plan doesn't come from an easy life, but from a life of suffering. We don't have to wait for our lives to "get better", or to be healed and whole; God is still working even when you can't see His purpose or plan.

The enemy will throw everything and anything at you to keep you from fulfilling God's purpose. But God will win that victory in your life because His purpose will stand firm. Remember, He has done it before, and He will do it again. Jesus and His promises are so much bigger and better than the darkness, so we need to lay down our worries and fears and trust Him with our life and our circumstances every day. It will take some work, and wholehearted trust in who God is and who He has shown that He is to you, but it will be worth it. He promises to never leave you nor forsake you, and He won't.

Your life isn't simply what you see, but it's what God sees. Sometimes we only see a fraction of our life; but God sees the whole picture. Colossians 1:17 says *"He is before all things, and in Him all things hold together."* We see a small piece of life, but God sees everything because He goes before us. Don't be frustrated because you only see a piece of your life, and maybe you don't like what you see. God sees the beginning, middle, and end. It's all beautiful to Him because it's your life, and it's all going according to His perfect plan. Again, He won't leave you or forsake you, ever.

I had to trust and hold onto the fact that God still had amazing things in store for me, even though I was in the midst of my grief. There wouldn't be a timeline for having a better handle on life. I didn't feel excited to serve, or to be challenged, or to watch God move in the lives of others, but I still wanted to pursue sharing the gospel. God knew all of that, He knew my pain and my frustration. He knew that I needed Him to move in my life, to be everything to me. I didn't have the strength or desire for anything else but Him. It felt like I was losing my passion for life, because my desires were gone in an instant. I didn't really know how to deal with that and be okay with this change of heart, but God was not surprised by any of it. He still had purpose and passion in store for me even though I struggled to see it.

We are meant to live a life of purpose and meaning, and when suffering enters your story, that doesn't necessarily stop. Our purpose in life may get a little hidden by the grief, so it might take some time to walk through the haze and fog of suffering to find our place in life again. But God reminds us that the suffering we will face in this life is part of our purpose on this earth. He says in 2 Corinthians 12:9, *"My grace is sufficient for you, for my power is made perfect in weakness."*

Suffering produces intimacy, Christlikeness, and a fulfilled life. When we are weak, He gives us His strength to persevere. Through that vulnerable relationship with God, we grow in intimacy with Him. As His love and grace for us brings us closer to Him, others are drawn to God as well when they see how we live our life. That is our purpose, to show others Jesus and bring them to Him. The apostle Paul lived a life of suffering and considered all that he gained in this life, as loss without Jesus. But with Jesus, his life was gain — including suffering. Intimacy, Christlikeness, and fulfillment do not come without suffering. Suffering is a blessing because of what it produces. Our life is only purpose-filled because of Christ, and the work He has done and continues to do in and through us. We learn that truth even more through our suffering because we can share with others the power and truth of what God has done in our lives.

Vulnerability in Hard Spaces

A couple months after my dad died, I had the opportunity to travel to Guatemala on a mission trip to spend time with some vulnerable kids who had suffered various types of traumas in their home and were living at a Christian orphanage. While I was there, God began to teach me a lot about the effects of trauma that kids can experience when they've been neglected and abused. Almost as soon as I met the children, my heart connected deeply with them and broke for the stories they had lived through. My grief took on another form, as I was constantly filled with compassion and empathy for these kids. As I desired to connect with them, the raw hurts that their stories exposed immediately drew me closer to them. I would experience a feeling similar to the way I had felt when hearing about families who had lost a loved one due to a terminal illness. Once again, that burning in my heart returned, just as painful and uncomfortable as it felt back when I first experienced it in Spain.

God was reminding me that He calls us to be the broken guiding the broken to Jesus. It was heartbreaking, but necessary, to realize the significance in this discovery of my growing passion for God's people. He has to show us how broken we are, so we understand how much we need Him in our lives. God uses our brokenness to highlight the work of the gospel; and He uses His love for us to encourage us and to encourage those who hear our stories. God uses the broken and unhealed parts of our stories to bring the broken to Christ. He doesn't call us to have it all together. He just calls us to share our story with others.

If we aren't trusting Jesus in all things, especially in the midst of our suffering, then we are not allowing ourselves to suffer with Him. We are just suffering alone. Without trusting in Him to be there with you, that suffering may feel everlasting and endlessly painful. But with Christ and His promise to never leave you nor forsake you, suffering can bring hope, renewal, joy, His eternal love, and intimacy with Him. True intimacy with the Father means trusting Him for the things you are mourning on this earth. We can't go through our suffering without Him, we need Him. Sometimes I forget that in the midst of my suffering, I can pour out the love of God to others as I share my story with them — the story He gave me.

You need to trust God for the mourning and sorrow you feel. Give those concerns to God, trust Him to work in your heart, and trust that He will use your suffering for His glory in beautiful ways. Everything you are and everything you go through in this life is a testament to God. If you feel compelled to dig deeper and listen to someone else's story, speak life and love into their story, or even share yours with them.

Significant Days in Another Season of Loss

Celebrating both of my parents' birthdays when they were both in heaven was truly heartbreaking to experience that first year. My dad's birthday is August 3rd and my mother's birthday is August 4th, so for that first year, the grief was unbearable. I missed them terribly and my heart literally hurt and ache. The pain felt twice as deep that year than when I was just celebrating my mother's birthday without her. But even in my sorrow, my dependance on God continued to grow.

It hurt not to have my dad with me, but I knew I needed to choose to rejoice. God's glory and good never ceased to be present in every part of my grief. As I kept feeling the intensity of having lost two amazing parents, the sorrow stuck around. It was hard to miss them both. The two people I cherished the most were gone. It was devastating, and at times, it literally took my breath away to think about them not being with me.

My mother's birthday hit different that year. It had been twelve years without her, and it was the first year without my dad. They both had left this earth, and they both had gone to heaven. It blew my mind to think that I had spent twelve years with my mother, and twelve years without her. The grief didn't feel like a wave that year, but like I was constantly drowning. My mother was my best friend. She and my dad accepted me and all of my quirks because they had them too — I loved that about them. At that point, my memories of her felt so far away, which only made me miss her even more. And missing my dad for the first time made it feel like I was losing my mother all over again. It felt like so much to carry, but I knew to rely on the strength of the Lord to make it through those especially hard days.

After celebrating those birthdays, grief pretty much blew up and didn't really leave me for a while. Crying out to God would happen in short bursts, and sometimes the tears never stopped — it felt like I was drowning. Other times, the grief lasted longer, and I would feel trapped in this darkness. But I knew God was there with me, holding me and waiting out the storm with me.

In my isolated moments of grief, a tidal wave of sorrow would come crashing into my subconscious, leaving me with this dull pain of weariness and defeat that I wore like a weighted blanket. When I chose to be alone, grief felt like I was in quicksand. Sometimes I wanted to get out and ask for help from others. But other times I did want to be stuck there, where I could sink a little, stay in bed, and be unmotivated to do life for a bit. God was there with me in those moments too. His constant presence is what kept me going and kept pushing me to get back up to continue doing life when it would've been so much easier to stop. Each morning, I knew I had to choose to get back up with God and go to the next moment He had in front of me.

The most impactful part of my grief journey this time, was that my hope, and dependance on God was never changing. I could make it through every painful moment because of Him. He wouldn't give me more than I could handle. He knew what each day would bring. He knew my strength, or lack thereof, and I could lean on the strength that He would provide me with for that day. I knew I needed to approach each day one moment at a time, knowing God would be right there with me every second.

But I wasn't always confident in my grief, because, at times, the fear would set back in when I started to dwell on the fact that I wasn't the same person I used to be before my dad died. I knew I wasn't the same joyful, giving-110%-in-everything-I-did kind of person like I was before. It was especially hard to come to terms with the fact that I wasn't able to give everything to my job at the nursing home anymore, and being surrounded by more death at work became too much to bear. So, with a heavy heart, I quit my job and temporarily stepped into a new job that required less of me emotionally.

But God was also calling me to be the emotionally raw person I was for that season. He knew the emotions had to constantly be written on my face to those around me, because He was also calling some of the people around me to see my emotions and respond in the exact way that I needed. I needed to be okay with the idea that I would likely never be that other person again. I needed to be okay with not knowing when I would stop feeling the depth of this grief, because I had no clue when things may or may not be going back to "normal" for me.

Grief broke me so many times over and over again. Experiences like loss and tragedy define you. They change you exactly how God designs them to. He created me to be the person I was in my grief, and I needed to be okay with that. God was calling me to redefine what it meant to be a child of God, a daughter of the King. His constant presence reassured me that He would be with me in every single moment He presented in my life, I just had to trust Him.

21 LEARNING TO LOVE MY GRIEF

There came a point and time in my recent journey of loss where I felt ready to give my grief the time and space to be held. Compared to when I lost my mother, I was ready and willing to face my grief instead of running from it. I wanted God to provide opportunities and people that would force me to face it. A few months after my dad died, life went on like normal, and it seemed like everyone around me had moved on. Only my close friends were present and still checking in on me, and I was very fortunate and thankful for them because most of the time it felt like I was alone in my grief.

So, I decided to reach out to our counseling ministry at church and get some insight into how I could analyze my grief. It still felt dark and isolating like before, but I had the truth of the gospel to quickly bring me back to the hope of Christ. I wanted to be sure that my lack of interest for life was normal, and that the moments of deep despair where I wanted God to take me home to Heaven so I could be with my parents, was a "normal" feeling.

During the couple sessions of counseling I had signed up for, I was encouraged to replace any negative thoughts I had with positive thoughts, and to speak scripture out loud. If I placed myself, by name, in scripture it would help to combat my negative mindset. The scripture of truth that helped me stay grounded with God's perspective on my life was Ephesians 6:10-15,

"Finally be strong in the Lord and in His mighty power. Put on the full armor of God so that you (Meena) can take your stand against the devil's schemes. For our strength is not against flesh and blood, but against the rulers, against the authorities, against the powers of the

dark world and against the spiritual forces of evil in the heavenly realms. Therefore, put on the full armor of God. So that when the day of evil comes, you may be able to stand your ground. And after you (Meena) have done everything to stand, stand firm then. With the belt of truth buckled around your waist, with the breastplate of righteousness in place, and with your feet fitted with the readiness that comes from the gospel of peace."

When staying positive and hopeful was hard, I needed to remember that I had the mind of Christ within me. We have all that we need to do what God has called us to do. My perspective on life needed to shift to be God's perspective on my life. I needed to start my day asking God, *what do you have for me today?* Every day it was also important for me to find ways to be thankful, even if it was just the birds and trees. The more consuming my grief felt, the humbler and full of grace I needed to be.

In the midst of grief, it's hard to take care of yourself, but God does. God is our strength when we feel weak. We are broken, but He makes us whole. Though we are still hurting, and our hearts are suffering, God is there with us. Surrender your brokenness and despair to Him. We may want the pain to end when our loss is still fresh, but we need to remember that God has promised to stick by us through it all. His love for us extends to understanding our pain and walking through it with us. He will be anything and everything we need in our toughest moments. We are utterly lost and hopeless without God.

Joy and Sorrow

In the fall of 2018, my church hosted a women's conference, and I was able to meet this incredible author, and now friend, Lindsey Dennis, and hear her incredible story of loss and redemption. I was able to share my story with her, and had the opportunity to read her book, *Buried Dreams*.

I was reminded through reading her book that our suffering is not without purpose, there is deliverance in our suffering. The Bible shows us many examples of God coming for His people in the midst of their suffering. He has not left us alone. *Even if it doesn't make sense, will you trust God? Will you remind yourself of His faithfulness?*

There is joy and thankfulness in sorrow. Don't let mourning overtake your heart. See God's grace for you displayed in His blessings, big and small. *What do you have to be thankful for? What blessings has He given you today?*

God's goodness and love for us is so consistently evident in and through each and every one of us, and I needed that reminder regularly. He walks with you in the good and bad. No matter what the day brings or how you're feeling, know that He is with you, right by your side, and that He goes before you. Every second of every day. Never doubt His love for you. You don't have to be perfect, or have it all together, to be completely and unconditionally loved by your Heavenly Father. That is where we have joy connected to our sorrow, joy in our mourning. Joy doesn't hide the fact that you are in sorrow; God sees where you're at and He says, *"It's okay my child. You don't have to feel okay. It's okay not to be okay, I will take care of you, you don't have to worry. Rest in me."*

He says that He is orchestrating something that we will not see. Hope in the things of this world is good, but doesn't compare to the hope that He is promising in eternity. Romans 8:18-27 says, *"patiently hope in what the Lord has promised, not for things in this world but for things to come."* Our grief is one piece of a greater story God is writing.

Your life may feel like it isn't moving but God is. Habakkuk 1 says, *"How long, o Lord? He declared. How long must I go on living like this? How long?"*[34] This was my heart's cry, at the core of myself. *"Because I am doing something in your days — you would not believe if you were told."*[35] God reminds us that He is at work, that He is still doing something.

Let God in and see what He wants to bring to the surface. God invites us to be vulnerable with Him, and to accept the reality of the suffering we are experiencing. He wants to be present with us in our suffering, He gives us grace and love. I felt like God saw me and was telling me, *"This is you. My best, my beautiful work of you. Your pain, your joy it's all my beautiful creation and art. You may not see it, but you are beautiful, and you are exactly who I created and loved, right here and now."* He takes us as we are, broken and whole. God doesn't call us to have it all together. His love isn't dependent on whether we get it right. God loves us the same when we succeed *and* when we fail. I found a lot of truth and comfort in scripture as I sought to understand this season of grief.

Jesus knows our grief because He Himself experienced grief, so He has compassion on us in our worst moments. He has compassion on us and understands us, so we can trust Him with our grief.[36]

God encourages us to not lose hope, because we have an eternal hope in Him. Our sufferings don't compared to the glory we have yet to experience. We as children of God wait in patience for the hope that we do not see. In our weakness, the Spirit has been given to us to intercede on our behalf to the Father when we don't have the words. God is with us and for us, and He wants to be near to us in our moments of grief and lament.[37]

In Acts 27, the apostle Paul emphasizes the importance of trusting God's promises in the midst of your storms, no matter the difficulty of your circumstances. You never know when God is going to place you in someone else's life to impact them through the gospel working in you. Your commitment to have faith during the storms of life is as much for you, as it is for those around you. God is working in you in those moments. Have faith when fear surrounds you, and when it's clouding your perception of what God is doing in you. His light will always shine in the darkness. He says in scripture, *"there will be trouble in this world, but take heart for I have overcome the world."*[38] Continuing to live life in the midst of overwhelming grief and death is a fight, but God calls us to surrender the burdens of this world to Him — releasing everything to the open arms of Jesus.

A New Normal

As the new year (2019) was approaching, I desperately wanted the next year of my life to be good; not marred by tragedy, just waiting for the next storm in my life to hit. I wanted to experience new things in life and grow closer to God, to my friends, and to my family. I wanted to be brave and bold, fearlessly trusting God for what He had in store for me next. My calling to ministry had started to feel clear again as my desires and dreams were slowly coming back. I just needed to be patient that God would bring it all to fruition.

By January of 2019, and in God's impeccable timing, He provided me with a job at Mosaic surrounded by church family, where I could grieve and grow in a place I already called home.

As I stepped further into the calling God had begun to place on my heart the more involved with ministry I became, I needed to redefine how I pursued Him and how I sought deeper intimacy with Him. I had been silent and kind of stagnant in my pursuit of God since my dad had died. I had loved pursuing Him in the past, but for a while I had lost a desire for His intimacy. I needed to learn how to pursue Him in the midst of my sorrow and pain. The hard work of enduring ongoing suffering wasn't done yet because my grief hadn't gone away, it had only grown.

I knew that falling in love with God and receiving His joy, while still suffering in my grief would take time. I needed to keep reminding myself to be patient and have grace upon grace for myself. It was okay if it could only be a small start, but I deeply desired to keep moving forward.

Our present reality in this world is that we are constantly in a state of suffering, so as we face trials, we have permission to grieve. God doesn't expect us to just pick up and move on from our suffering. He asks us to keep living and to rejoice while we suffer, because He knows that through our grief, we can display the gospel and His love in a way that can only be explained by Him. God uses seasons of suffering to encourage us and others, because His presence and faithfulness is greatly displayed in our grief. His gift of the Holy Spirit at work within us demonstrates the genuineness of our faith. He uses our trials to show us how genuine our faith is because of His strength, peace, and perseverance at work within us. It is God who makes our faith genuine, not us.

Once we are in regular rhythms of crying out to God and trusting in His faithfulness to be present and to care for us in our struggles, we can learn to be hopeful and thankful for the present circumstances. Jeremiah 29:10-14 reminds us of a promised future hope,

> *"For thus says the Lord: When seventy years are completed for Babylon, I will visit you, and I will fulfill to you my promise and bring you back to this place. For I know the plans I have for you, declares the Lord, plans for welfare and not for evil, to give you a future and a hope. Then you will call upon me and come and pray to me, and I will hear you. You will seek me and find me, when you seek me with all your heart. I will be found by you, declares the Lord, and I will restore your fortunes and gather you from all the nations and all the places where I have driven you, declares the Lord, and I will bring you back to the place from which I sent you into exile."*

Our trials and suffering have purpose. Be encouraged. We can choose to be thankful for the present and ask God to help us pray boldly about the future He has promised us.

So much of my life would have given me permission to run away from God and everyone in my life. But, because of God's work in my life, I can stand firm and have joy. There are so many reasons to be thankful for this life we get to live, including the parts of life where suffering and loss don't seem to end. Thank you, Lord, for every moment, every beautiful and heart-wrenching moment of this life.

During the spring of 2019, I began to notice that my community and my friendships were looking a little different than they had months before. I felt a real loss within my community, and it wasn't anyone's fault. Life was just different and what I needed from others was different. I still had my friends, but at times, it felt like my life was going down a different path than theirs was. It felt incredibly isolating, and so I distanced myself further away from my friends. I couldn't seem to figure out my feelings.

But other times, I felt fine. That's what was so misleading to me. I would feel fine in one moment, feeling so blessed by the community around me. But in another moment, I would feel incredibly alone in my suffering. I wasn't ready to try counseling again, even though I knew that was the correct next step. I was beginning to fear that my grief was turning into the same grief as before, that it was close to becoming fueled by depression and seclusion. I was afraid that soon I would start avoiding my grief, and avoiding others, because I was already "so good" at pushing people away. It became easier to stop letting people in, and to avoid putting my vulnerabilities out there in a way that I knew I needed to.

But God's grace. Life is hard sometimes. Living a story of loss is exhausting. It's normal for life to take it out of you, even when you have God on your side. Breaking down felt like it was just around the corner some days, and for most of 2019 I was only able to live moment to moment. One minute I would feel fine, and the next I would be terrified just thinking about getting through the next day. I worried about desiring hopes and dreams for my future again, as the reality of losing those desires became too real to bear. Before my own eyes, I was a different person than I had been a year ago, and I didn't know how to live in that.

It was weird to have a new normal where my dad wasn't there anymore. I felt like the life around me should have ceased to exist, that no one should have been moving on without him. I knew my dad was right where he should be, in Heaven. Almost a year after his death, I was finally accepting that he was gone. My dad was right where God wanted him to be, and so I need to be sure that I was right where God needed me to be too.

A New Outlook on Counseling

I reached a point in my grief where I was having so many breakdowns in the middle of the day, that seemed to come out of nowhere. I would have a panic attack and then start sobbing uncontrollably, and I couldn't figure out why. I knew it was time to go back to counseling, but I didn't want it to be solely because I had lost two parents and needed help with my grief. Once I came to an understanding that counseling was an opportunity for me to learn about myself and learn how to process my emotions to live a healthier life, I was more accepting of the idea. It was very eye opening for me to learn about my emotions, my meta-emotions (feelings about my feelings), my self-judgments, and my self-assumptions. It was incredibly beneficial for me to learn how to understand myself better, instead of letting my emotions boil up and explode all the time. I knew and accepted that I needed counseling regularly to better understand myself and to be able to take better care of myself.

It was hard at first to sit in all my emotions with a kind, new stranger, but having constant grace and patience for myself made the process slightly easier. I struggled to avoid sinking into the trap of comparison as I started the journey of counseling. It was easy to ask myself, *"why me? why can't I have this other life?"*, or *"why is this so hard for me?"*. But that wasn't helping me move forward into health. I needed to appreciate the life God had given me.

Loss inevitably came up in counseling as well. So, we talked about how losing my parents held different levels of grief for me. Grief for my mother wasn't as painful anymore, it felt more like a dull feeling of mourning and lament — like my heart ached for her. Realizing that I had lived so many years of my life without her, constantly blew my mind. It's like I could vaguely remember my life with my mother and our memories. But I still wanted to avoid grieving her because I didn't want to live in the past and get stuck wishing for something that could never be — for her to be alive with me. Missing my mother and dwelling on her loss still felt like I had lost my best friend. That thought still made me want to run and keep running, and just outrun my entire life. The grief from losing my dad was still so new and painful anytime I thought about it, but that felt familiar and healthy to me.

The concept of having lost a parent was almost unfathomable to try to wrap my mind around. But to lose a mother, the one who gave me life, was irreparable to the heart. It was always hard to talk about her with other people, and it wasn't just that I was uncomfortable and didn't want to be sad. Years later, I still felt like I would be burdening others with having to care for me if I talked about my mother. Talking about my mother with my counselor was hard, but it felt more freeing because I knew she was used to hearing hard stories and it wouldn't be a burden for her. Our time together grew more freeing and enjoyable each time we met.

In my grief, I only ever want someone to sit with me, console me, love me, and encourage me. I rarely need advice, just a hug is enough or for someone to look me in the eye and tell me that they are there for me. Each time I share my story with someone for the first time, it's a reminder that Jesus makes my story beautiful, even if I don't always feel like it is.

Dad's Heaven-anniversary

Before I knew it, it was almost a year since my dad had died, and I wasn't ready to relive the memories of my life spent with him. But I knew that I needed to. It was hard to live my life remembering all the tragedy that had happened, even though I knew there was joy in it too.

But sometimes you just have to let yourself feel it, the tragedies and the joy. I didn't want to hide, deflect, or avoid, I wanted to feel it all. I needed to take the space and time to be sad, to be a little devastated, and to long and mourn the life lost and the memories that would never be.

Letting yourself feel the extent of your grief can be tragically beautiful. At one point, you may find yourself desiring so strongly to be with your loved ones who have passed. It's not like you are suicidal, but you do want to physically leave this earth for the purpose of being with your loved ones. This desire invokes the deep longing of our hearts to live in the new heaven and the new earth. As people of God, it's natural to want to be with our loved ones and not on this earth. When I would miss my mother and my dad and desire to be with them, I didn't long for them to be here with me on earth, because they truly are in a better place. This world continues to hold pain, suffering, and more death for them. They have received their eternal reward. So, I wouldn't wish for them to be come back. Instead, I'd wish that God could take me home so I could leave this life of suffering, pain, and death. Then I, too, could receive my eternal reward and be with my mother and my dad. I would have days where I deeply desired to just be where they are. This desperation felt like an ache in the depths of my heart that only God understood.

In the midst of initial grief, this longing can leave you feeling purposeless and hopeless. What is the purpose of being on this earth when all we want to do is be home with our loved ones? Why God, are we here and not them? What else do you have in store for me, especially in light of this profound loss? These are important questions to ask God because He does in fact have a purpose for you being on this earth while your loved ones are already called home.

Let those questions and longings point you back to Christ, and have others come alongside you and pray for you. It may feel isolating and weird to be having these thoughts, but they do come after loss. Life doesn't make a lot of sense after losing a loved one. Everything you thought you knew before is being questioned. You are at a loss to even do the simplest of tasks, and you may feel like you can't handle a lot on your own. So, what should do you to remedy that? You do have to function and exist right? You may have responsibilities like children, a spouse, or your job to be responsible for. Life around you does continue to keep moving.

When I asked God these questions, He would remind me of the importance of leaning on His strength, and not on my own. Trying to make sense of the constantly changing and broken world around me was exhausting. Even just existing after loss was draining. When my dad died, every breath and every movement required intentional thought. Just opening my eyes and getting out of bed was taxing. I literally didn't have my own strength to rely on, so, I had to start by asking God for help.

Pray for the strength to ask God for help. You have to start somewhere; no task or step is too small. God says that He won't ever leave you or forsake you. Let God's strength sustain and restore you, lean on Him. It's okay and human to not have the strength or heart to exist. There were times where smiling was exhausting and required actual effort. It was not enjoyable to be so limited in so many ways. But God needed me to stop and rest, to let Him take care of me in a way that no one else could. And in that space, I was actually able to let myself grieve.

First Peter 4:1-6 reminds us that in this life, we need to arm ourselves with Christ's way of thinking, so that we can endure the journey of redemption. When we are thinking in the mind of Christ, we will know without a doubt of the joy set before us. *"Fixing our eyes on Jesus, the pioneer and perfecter of faith. For the joy set before him he endured the cross, scorning its shame, and sat down at the right hand of the throne of God."* [39] God will help you remember why you are here, and where He is leading you next. Though everything looks different in light of grief, God is still the same God. Look ahead to the joy set before you, in Heaven. It takes utter dependance on Jesus alone. We have to submit ourselves to the work of the Holy Spirit and allow Him to direct and define our thinking and feeling. This inner transformation will then extend outwardly and affect how you continue to live your life. Our joy, purpose, and hope will no longer feel like a foreign concept or unattainable goal to achieve, but actual reality in our present lives. Once we come to the realization that we alone cannot change our perspective and our thinking, but only the gospel and only Jesus, then can we begin to move forward in healing.

Grief can be frustrating and exhausting, like you're constantly being drained from an empty well. If I could have asked myself how I was feeling about arriving at the one-year mark of my dad passing, I would have honestly said that I still felt a little hopeless and purposeless. I knew God had called me to proclaim His word and display the gospel in my life. But when I entered grief and thought of my personal story, at times, I still couldn't understand why I was here at all. What did I have to give to the kingdom of God with a story like mine?

Though I had learned a lot in the first year without my dad, I still felt broken and damaged. I still struggled to see the freedom, redemption, and peace in my story, but I could see it in the stories of others around me. Looking inward at my own life, it became hard to understand how God could love all of me, especially the parts that I didn't understand about myself. Even a year after loss I would walk around feeling utterly alone. Even though I was surrounded and loved, I felt forgotten about at the same time.

So, in those moments of doubt and longing, I would ask God to help me seek after Him with a burning passion and desire to know Him more. All I needed to get through this life, all I needed to feel loved, cared for, and affirmed, was God. After loss, it was like a spark died inside of me that used to ignite and fan the flame of my passion for God and His love. I used to desire God so much, but everything was different, and I often needed His help to rekindle that flame in my heart for Him.

Somehow by the time the day had actually arrived, May 28th, 2019, the worries that had been keeping me up before didn't seem to matter as much anymore. God reassured me that He would take care of everything. I could take on the next year without my loved ones who were gone and be bold and confident in what He was calling me to do and be. The redeeming spaces were still there, and I still needed God to refine me. Grief still had a lot to teach me.

The apostle Peter uses the beautiful name *beloved* in 1 Peter 4:12-19 to remind us that in the fiery trials God still loves us. When it feels like God isn't there, and that He's forgotten you, remember you are beloved. This "testing" that we are going through in our suffering, is refining and purifying us. Don't be surprised or discouraged, redeeming unredeemed spaces is hard. Refining Planet Death, as my pastor calls earth, is hard. We are not home yet.

When trials refine us within, they are also part of our mission to show the gospel to those around us. We are a light in the darkness of this world, and the people of this world who aren't saved, need to see God's light shining through us in our sufferings. The ungodly and the sinner can be redeemed by the work that God does in and through us. He knows what He is doing. Let Him use you, refine you, and redeem you for His kingdom and glory.

> *"And after you have suffered a little while, the God of all grace, who has called you to His eternal glory in Christ, will himself restore, confirm, strengthen, and establish you. Compared to eternity with God, our suffering will last but a moment, in light of eternity."*[40]

We bring about the beauty of the gospel when we look out for each other. Standing in the middle between the enemy and others. Stand firm in your faith together. Suffering can produce isolation, but you are not alone. Remember and know that the same kinds of suffering are being experienced by your brotherhood throughout the world.[41] You are not alone. Be strong and firm in your foundation. You will get through this. When we are being restored, our brokenness is being mended and our broken bones are being set. We will be able to stand the test of time and be filled with the strength of the Lord. God has promised that He will do all of this for us. When all is said and done, there is nothing more beautiful than the gospel at work in us. The story of God's love for us is more than we could ever deserve and yet is freely given. You story is a beautiful story of God's love.

22 NEW LIFE AFTER DEATH

The Beauty of Community

Life after death is strangely surreal. Suffering can feel so isolating, that at times you may feel alone, abandoned, and forgotten about. But if all of my past years of living with loss have taught me anything, it's that I am not alone. Sometimes it is hard to say those words, *"I need help"* out loud, and ask others to be there for you. But we have to trust those in our life and try. We need our community to heal.

My community was there for me in so many ways when my dad died, and I'll never have enough words to express how much they mean to me. In that first year, and many years afterward, my friends and family stood by me. When I didn't have the strength to even ask for help, they came alongside me. They held me and sat with me as I cried. They fed me and overwhelmed me with love and kindness. The kind of community I experienced, could only be described as a near perfect example of Christ's love — a picture of His church.

There is another image that a close friend of mine shares with me often when I am being too stubborn to ask her, or anyone, for help. She reminds me of the story in Exodus 17 when the people of Israel are fighting the nation of Amalek. In this chapter, Moses holds up his hands so that Israel would be victorious in the fight, but any time he lowered his hands, they failed. So as Moses' hands grew weary, Aaron and Hur came alongside of him, on his right and on his left, to hold up his hands so that Israel would prevail over Amalek. She reminds me of this story to emphasize the importance of sharing our burdens with one another — to hold each other's arms up when we are weary. God calls us to bear one another's burdens, the true honor we have in Godly friendship. Though it is a lesson I am constantly learning, I am truly blessed by the people God has placed in my life, and I am constantly thankful for their desire to hold my arms up when I am weak.

It's powerful to experience how God loves us through the way that others come alongside and love us in our suffering. It's a joy to experience Him moving in the lives of others as well, fellowship is a true joy given to us by God. In my suffering, God continued to stir in me a desire to love on others, by showing them the love of Jesus in the midst of their suffering.

When I felt like I had lost my passion and purpose in life after my dad died, I was reminded that my purpose in life is to further the gospel of Christ to those around me. My heart's desire for the rest of my days is to do just that, to connect with people profoundly and deeply, and to care for them and love them in all seasons of life. God had continued to stir within me a heart of mercy and empathy for the community around me.

Though it was painful at times, to be in the same sorrowful space with others because I felt their emotions almost as strongly as they did, I knew once again that it was a gift that God had given me. This gift of empathy had always been inside of me, I just wasn't ready to accept it and live it out until now. Once I had truly begun to heal and accept my grief as a gift and as a blessing, not as a burden, then I could finally appreciate my heart of empathy. God had done so much for me, and now I could love my story and my suffering. He had given me the most beautiful passion and purpose, to share my story of God's love so that others could see His love in their stories too. I was beginning to learn to love this spiritual gift of mercy that was flourishing right before my eyes. I finally felt ready to seek and pursue the dreams that God had begun to put on my heart.

By the end of 2019 I had lost so many people in my community, losses that truly rocked the earth beneath me. But I knew that God would be faithful again, I had no choice but to believe that. I had to trust that He would make these losses beautiful because that is the kind of God He is. I desperately needed Him to use me to be His vessel because my empathy felt overwhelming. I constantly felt the emotions of others, their tragedies, and their stories that felt so much like my own. God drew me closer to Himself in those moments. He allowed me to be filled so that I could love and care for others, in hopes of bringing them closer to Jesus to heal their hearts as

He had healed mine. Death and loss are inevitable, but the pain I felt in my heart just seemed to emphasize the fact that I had loved so many so well in my life.

Right after Christmas Day, a close friend of mine at my church left this earth to be with Jesus, and her death hurt deeply like so many of the other losses had before. She was a true angel, someone brought into my life by God Himself. She meant the world to me. She had walked me through losing my dad and had helped me learn how to take time for myself. I truly looked up to her as she guided me in strengthening my spiritual life. She knew when my heart was burdened, and I loved processing my grief with her. She even let me spend the first anniversary of my dad's death with her at her beach house. She met with me regularly, listened to me, and loved me and others so well. She never missed an opportunity to share God's word with those around her as she was so in tune with the Holy Spirit.

I had the opportunity to see her in the hospital before she passed, even though it brought back some memories I struggled to relive from visiting my mother in the hospital. It was so special to be able to talk to her, pray over and with her, and sing to her. The time that myself and others were able to spend worshiping with her was precious. I loved every minute of it and could feel the peace and presence of God in the room. I thank God for allowing me the chance to be there to love on her and say goodbye to her. The holidays were difficult that year as the loss and sorrow was so profound in our community.

My community went through so much loss that year, a close friend lost her sister, we all lost a member of our church staff, another friend lost her baby, loss was everywhere. I didn't want to lose more people, but I knew I would continue to.

I don't want the people I love to leave this earth, but I know they must go home when God calls them. Celebrating in hard circumstances is a battle, and sometimes we have to fight to celebrate.[42] I've experienced so many deep losses as the people who've really impacted and shaped my life have left this earth. In the beginning of my seasons of grief and lament, I always question everything, no matter how sure I am of God's promises for my life.

But God. He always brings me out of my pit of sinking grief, and I always believe the love He has for me. It's good to feel my grief, but it's painful, dark, mournful, and full of melancholy. It's raw, real, and all-encompassing. When my grief overflows, I feel like I'm grieving all of my losses and empathizing with everyone around me who is grieving at the same time. It's draining. But it's beautiful when God shows me what He can do with all my grief. I know He will use it for good, because He has done that for me in the past. So, whenever I grieve and emote strongly with others, I pray that God will let me feel as much as I need to, with the space to also encourage others, trusting that He will bring joy, strength, and healing for me as well.

I am thankful for every single tear I shed because they are necessary and beautiful. They tell a story of heartache and found peace; stories of a girl turned woman who survived and keeps living on, who dreams and strives to be more tomorrow. I hope that I keep crying forever, not tears of prolonged anguish, but of renewed hope.

Even the days where suffering and grief threaten to swallow you whole, persist and persevere to find the joy in your life. Find God. Seek Him out. Cry out to Him. The only purpose you need in this life is to be with God. He will sustain you when your whole world is crumbling around you *and* when you have reasons to celebrate. He is present in all circumstances and will sit with you as you weep *and* as you rejoice.

One of my favorite books is called *Hinds Feet in High Places* by Hannah Hurnard, and I want to leave you with the last section of the book to dwell on. As the main character, Much-Afraid (who symbolizes all of us at the beginning of our journey with Christ), finally reaches the High Places (a place of spiritual growth and maturity) after her long journey of discovering who she is as a new creation in the Lord, as a beloved child of God, she takes some time to reflect on all that she has learned from the Shepherd (God).

> *"At last she put her hand in his and said softly, 'My Lord, I will tell you what I learned.' 'Tell me,' he answered gently. 'First,' said she, 'I learned that I must accept with joy all that you allowed to happen to me on the way and everything to which the path led me! That I was never to try to evade it but to accept it and lay down my own will on the altar and say, 'Behold me, I am thy little handmaiden Acceptance-with-Joy.' Then I learned that I must bear all that others were allowed to do against me and to forgive with no trace of bitterness and to say to thee, 'Behold me — I am thy little handmaiden Bearing-with-Love,' that I may receive power to bring good out of this evil.' The third thing I learned was that you, my Lord, never regarded me as I actually was,*

lame and weak and crooked and cowardly. You saw me as I would be when you had done what you promised and had brought me to the High Places, when it could be truly said, 'There is none that walks with such a queenly ease, nor with such grace, as she.' You always treated me with the same love and graciousness as though I were a queen already and not wretched little Much-Afraid.' Then she looked up into his face and for a little time could say no more, but at last she added, 'My Lord, I cannot tell you how greatly I want to regard others in the same way.' 'The fourth thing was really the first I learned up here. Every circumstance in life, no matter how crooked and distorted and ugly it appears to be, if it is reacted to in love and forgiveness and obedience to your will can be transformed. Therefore I begin to think, my Lord, you purposely allows us to be brought into contact with the bad and evil things that you want changed. Perhaps that is the very reason why we are here in this world, where sin and sorrow and suffering and evil abound, so that we may let you teach us so to react to them, that out of them we can create lovely qualities to live forever. That is the only really satisfactory way of dealing with evil, not simply binding it so that it cannot work harm, but whenever possible overcoming it with good."[43]

CONCLUSION

Over the years, I've come to know God in such a unique way through my suffering. And I can honestly say that I wouldn't change any part of my life at all. My suffering and my losses have made me who I am today. They have broken, renewed, weakened, and strengthened me to be the woman of God I am today. My love and devotion to God is truly stronger because of the life I have lived and continue to live.

I have had this dream to write a book about my life, thus far, for many years. But I needed to wait until now to write it. As much as I thought it was because I wasn't ready and didn't have the skills or creativity to write, it was because God was telling me to be patient as He was healing my story and my heart. I am so grateful to Him for that. How I see the world is vastly different now because of God's work and display of love in my life. As God provided more opportunities to share what He was doing in my life, through the people I encountered to writing blogs about my adventures in Spain, the passion to live my life sharing His love through suffering and loss grew. It became the only aspiration and purpose in my life that I knew without a shadow of a doubt God had blessed me with. My heart and passion for His people grew more and more as I shared my story, and as I heard the stories of loss of any and all kinds from other people.

I want to leave you all, my readers, with one last thing as I finish sharing my story. I used to think that only one tragic thing could happen in each of our lives. I thought that we could really only handle one tragedy, one death, one loss. But after I lost my dad four and a half years ago, I knew that was not true. After coming to know the Lord intimately and deeply in the midst of my grief, I came to understand that God is still a good God, even though I had suffered another loss. He is not a god who enjoys our suffering or is just sitting on the sidelines watching us suffer. He is a loving and kind God who is saddened by our suffering and wants to come alongside us and holds us.

The suffering we experience in this life is all because of result of sin and death in this world we live in. Suffering exists because we live in a broken world and are broken people. Our world is full of sin, and suffering will not end while we are in this world. Coming to terms with the reality of this world and the reality of the love of God was the only way that I could begin to survive loss again. My world had been shattered four and a half years ago, and my worst fear had come true. But God was not surprised by my loss. He was ready and able to carry me, my family, and friends in our suffering, because that's the kind of God He is. He knows that until the new heaven and new earth come after all have heard of His salvation and love, we will suffer, and we will have to say goodbye to our loved ones before we are ready. Can you ever be "ready" to say goodbye to someone you love? Whether they leave this earth as a newborn, as a child, as a young adult, or as an elderly relative? No. Loss is unimaginable no matter the age of the person you lost. How they died is tragic no matter the type of circumstance. And if you've lost a person, a relationship, or a way of life, your suffering is significant too.

If your life has drastically changed and has caused you to question your identity, purpose, and reason for living, I'm sorry. I know things will never be the same, and that you will need some time to get your bearings. Take that time. Be gracious to yourself, please. And know that your Creator, your Heavenly Father, sees your pain and empathizes completely with you. He is here for you and will not leave your side. Trust me.

While we are on this earth our suffering will not end, but our God is sovereign and faithful to keep His promises to sustain, strengthen, and uphold you. He loves you deeply and unconditionally. I urge you to discover what that love is for yourself. Discover who God is, and what He means when He says, *"I will never leave you nor forsake you."*[44] Read the Bible, lament with scripture written for you, and find the peace that passes all understanding. He is waiting for you.

Thank you for reading my story, it truly means the world to me that I can share my journey with you. This story is so precious to me, and it has shown me so much about our God and how He cares for us in our suffering. In His love for me and devotion to be present and graciously kind in my suffering, He has brought me unexplainable joy. Joy in living this life in the midst of grief. Joy in the depths of despair because of His insurmountable love for His people. Joy in the everyday as I appreciate His creation. Joy in my weakness and struggles. Simply, joy in Him.

ACKNOWLEDGMENTS

I want to thank my mom, Nancy, for being the best mom I could ask for, you are an exemplary woman of God, and I am forever thankful to be your daughter. Jaq, Ashley, Breshia, Jamie, James, Jermaine, Enoch, Ezra, and Josiah, thank you for always being home for me and consistently showing me that our dad is never gone from our hearts.

I want to thank so many of my close friends, too many to name but you know who you are. Many of you sat with me in the depths of my grief and didn't leave my side, and you still fight for my joy. You bring me closer to God each and every day. I will never be able to thank you enough for loving me so well.

Thank you to my editors, Nancy Rivera, Annika Hedstrom-Reeder, and Crisilee DeBacker, for the hard work you dedicated to editing this book. Thank you to Kevin Richardson for creating and perfecting the cover of this book, you are a master at this craft among many others. And thank you to my close friends and supporters, Emily Ward, Victoria Borgela, Maddie Lane, Seth Kaye, Hannah and Jordan Busekrus, Hannah South, Summer Darnell, Tricia Ruiz, Annika and Zach Reeder, Jen and Kevin Richardson, and Lindsey Dennis who encouraged me and gave me advice throughout my writing journey. Thank you to everyone I work with at Mosaic, all of my siblings, my entire extended family, and really the entirety of my church and my local and global community for cheering me on for the last two and a half years as I worked on this. You all greatly contributed to making this book possible.

Lastly, I want to thank you, my readers, because whether you know it or not, you are light in this world. God loves you, and He loves the story He has written for you. I want you to find and share your own story. The world is waiting, and God is ready to help you take that step.

ABOUT THE AUTHOR

Meena Rivera graduated from Palm Beach Atlantic University with a Bachelor's Degree in Business Administration and currently resides in Clermont, Florida. She works at a church in Winter Garden and is passionate about caring for others and stepping into hard stories of grief with her family, friends, and community.

NOTES

CHAPTER 7: AN UNWELCOME REALITY CHECK
[1] Ps. 139:13-16

CHAPTER 12: FOUNDATIONS OF INTIMACY WITH GOD
[2] Rev. 21:1-4

CHAPTER 13: GROWING TRUST AND FAITH
[3] Gen. 22:1-19, Gen. 17:15-21
[4] Pete Scazzero. *Emotionally Healthy Spirituality* (Zondervan, 2017), 24.
[5] Pete Scazzero. *Emotionally Healthy Spirituality* (Zondervan, 2017), 24.
[6] Pete Scazzero. *Emotionally Healthy Spirituality* (Zondervan, 2017), 79.

CHAPTER 14: DOES THE ENEMY HAVE A FOOTHOLD
[7] Rom. 12:1-2
[8] Pete Scazzero. *Emotionally Healthy Spirituality* (Zondervan, 2017), 89.
[9] Pete Scazzero. *Emotionally Healthy Spirituality* (Zondervan, 2017), 79.
[10] Pete Scazzero. *Emotionally Healthy Spirituality* (Zondervan, 2017), 50.
[11] Jam. 4:6-10
[12] Rom. 12:1-20
[13] Rom. 8

CHAPTER 15: DEEPER DEVELOPMENT
[14] Col. 3:2
[15] Isa. 53:4-5
[16] Deut. 31:6

CHAPTER 16: WHEN YOU CAN'T MAKE SENSE OF YOUR OWN GRIEF
[17] Pete Scazzero. *Emotionally Healthy Spirituality* (Zondervan, 2017), 126.
[18] Pete Scazzero. *Emotionally Healthy Spirituality* (Zondervan, 2017), 133.
[19] 1 Thess. 4:13-18

CHAPTER 17: HEALING AND REDEEMING THE DEEPEST WOUNDS
[20] Mayo Clinic Staff. "Depression (major depressive disorder)". Mayo Clinic. October 14, 2022. https://www.mayoclinic.org/diseases-conditions/depression/symptoms-causes/syc-20356007#:~:text=Visit%20mayoclinic.org.,of%20emotional%20and%20physical%20problems.
[21] 1 Jn. 4:18
[22] Phil. 4:4-9
[23] Psa. 100

[24] Rom. 8:26
[25] Matt. 18:31-35
[26] Lk. 6:27-36
[27] Rom. 8
[28] Rom. 12:2
[29] Jn. 16:33

CHAPTER 19: LIFE IN MINISTRY
[30] 2 Cor. 4:16-18
[31] 2 Cor. 4:3-6
[32] 2 Cor. 16-18

CHAPTER 20: WHEN MY WORLD STOPPED MOVING
[33] Col. 1:17

CHAPTER 21: LEARNING TO LOVE MY GRIEF
[34] Hab. 1:2
[35] Hab. 1:5b
[36] Isa. 53:3-5
[37] Rom. 8:18-27
[38] Jn. 16:33
[39] Heb. 12:2
[40] 1 Pet. 5:10
[41] 1 Pet. 5:9

CHAPTER 22: NEW LIFE AFTER DEATH
[42] Psa. 145:14-21
[43] Hannah Hurnard. *Hinds' Feet on High Place*s (Tyndale House, 1975) 121-122.
[44] Deut. 31:6

Made in the USA
Middletown, DE
08 January 2023

21680475R00099